# From Blitz to Glitz

The autobiography of
## Jess Conrad

Written with

## Simon Withington

Forewords by
## Jim Davidson & Rick Wakeman

**OAK TREE BOOKS**

First published in 2024 by
**Oak Tree Books**
oaktreebooks.uk

an imprint of
**Andrews UK Limited**
West Wing Studios
Unit 166, The Mall
Luton, LU1 2TL
United Kingdom
andrewsuk.com

Discography compiled by Graham Hunter, with great thanks.

*To Renée, my wife of sixty years*

*and my mum, who would have been*
*so proud of her boy writing his own book.*

# Contents

# Included Photographs

# Foreword

## *by Jim Davidson*

It was 1974. I had made it through to the final of a talent contest organised by a brewery called *Trumans*. The venue was the Lyceum in the West End of London. There were a number of categories that were being judged, mine of course, was comedy. I stuck my head around the side of the stage to look at the audience and more importantly the judges. One judge stood out; he was head and shoulders above the rest, literally. He was the most handsome man I'd ever seen and looked every inch a star, something I wanted desperately to be.

I came second in the comedy section and went backstage desperately sad, getting a cuddle from my mother. In walked the charismatic judge. He made a beeline for me, shook my hand and told me how wonderful I was. He told me I was going to be a star. I remember asking him , "How do I get what you have?" He replied, "What? These two birds?" (He had a brace of gorgeous models with him). I told him that I was talking about his charisma. I will never forget what he told me; he said, "You've got it son; don't you worry about that." He gave me hope. He made me feel special. His name was Jess Conrad.

Jess is a very special human being. He is generous and kind, but most of all he is funny. He sends himself up something rotten. I love the man and always will. If I had to pick guests for a dinner party, Jess would be the first phone call. He has so many stories and is a delight to listen to. So, sit back and read some of those stories and you will love him too.

# Foreword

## *by Rick Wakeman*

I can honestly say that Jess is one of my dearest friends, and it's been a privilege to have been involved in quite a few of them, and those that I haven't, to have been able to collapse in hysterical laughter witnessing them from afar.

It's often said that it's important to love yourself and with no difficulty whatsoever, Jess has certainly achieved this. At a lunch with him and Renée, in a lovely Italian restaurant near *Pinewood Studios*, my wife Rachel asked Renée what the secret was of their long marriage, and she simply replied, "It's easy. We're both in love with the same man."

He ran the Top 10 XI and the Showbiz XI football teams which were a riot. We played at some great stadiums (Molineux, Craven Cottage and Wembley Stadium to name but a few), and also some crap ones, but we didn't care. Jess ran it all properly. We had great kits and a sponge man, and we had a Showbiz XI car, a Ford Granada if I recall. Actually, we didn't have the sponsored car, Jess did!

Jess was our goalkeeper, and to be fair, a pretty good one too, but whereas most goalkeepers took out a towel and gloves with them onto the pitch, Jess took a mirror and comb, and whenever a penalty was awarded, he'd spend at least ten minutes doing his hair and checking the make-up (which was known to us all as a *mirror check*), and then tell the penalty taker which way he always dived so that the photographers would get his best side. Amazingly, he saved a load of these penalties, but the photos were always strange as Jess never looked for the ball, just smiled into the camera lens.

In later years as we all got older, football became golf, which did present some difficulty for Jess, as when addressing the ball on the tee he never really knew how to look down the fairway in order for photographers to get his best side. He played in loads of charity golf tournaments for Sparks and the Variety Club, and at my Sparks event at Burgh Hill we made a new local rule that any golfer was allowed a free drop if it landed in or near any of Jess's makeup.

He loved to sing at events and functions and people truly loved him, and still do, and indeed so do all his fellow entertainers. *Be Bop a Lula* became a staple at every after-dinner event that I ever went to!

In 2013 the *Grand Order of Water Rats* made Jess King Rat and he kindly asked me to be his Prince Rat for the year, a privilege of which I greatly enjoyed as I then went on to become King Rat myself, which would not have happened without Jess asking me to take the office of Prince Rat in his year.

Most importantly, Jess is, to all of us in the entertainment industry, a total one-off who we all love dearly. He always calls me "Trick", and so that's how I will sign off this foreword. So readers, prepare to put a smile on your face as you enjoy a great read.

Trick.

*Dad, mum and a young Gerry boy on the beach in Hastings*

# 1: War Years

I'm a South London boy, a true Cockney born within the sound of Bow Bells at the General Lying-In Hospital in Kennington. I was born Gerald Arthur James on 24th February 1936, which makes me a Pisces.

We lived in Herne Hill, and one of my first memories as a baby is being under a table and hearing my mother say, "He'll be out in a minute," and I'd crawl out from the table, and they'd all applaud, and I'd just sit there and not know what to do. Although they seemed happy enough for me just to sit there and look good. Later in life, I always made sure I looked good, knew my lines and was always well-prepared so I had something to do.

My mother's name was Linda Knight, she spelt it with a 'y' as she thought it looked posher. She had five brothers, and was a South London beauty queen who looked very much like a film star of the time, Linda Darnell. My father was a jazz pianist, a great fan of the Fats Waller & Cab Calloway, and was in a band called The Night Owls. One of the songs he used to sing was *Nobody Loves you 'cos your feet's too big* (Oh, your feet's too big, don't want you 'cause you feet's too big. Mad at you 'cause your feet's too big, I hate you 'cause your feet's too big.) And, incidentally, I take a size 11! He played the piano, as did his mother, and because of it was the star of the family until many years later I came along and took the limelight. Dad was called up and became a military policeman for the Secret Service and was stationed in Iceland, and I remember seeing pictures of him on a motorbike. To cheer him up, I went to the local photography

*Lynda, my mother*

1

*Ready for war*

shop and dressed up as I thought a soldier should look and posted him a picture.

One of my early memories, when I heard the air raid siren, which was a distinctive sound, was that I would go out onto the road and watch them dropping their bombs, not realising I could get killed. But all the lights and hullabaloo were very exciting.

During the war, most wives did something to help the war effort. As dad was overseas in the army, mum became an ambulance driver, so for a time I lived at 123 New Church Road, Camberwell with my grandma, who we called Fatty Nan. Cockneys have all these names for people, I suppose that is the reason why I have codenames for all my friends now (Kenny Lynch was always Kipper, Jim Davidson is The General etc.). At that time, there were no husbands around because of the second world war, so it was just me and mum. In those days we would go from Brixton to Camberwell and see Fatty Nan, which was a fair walk, past the King's College Hospital on Denmark Hill. My grandad was always there. He was a baker, originally from Guernsey, of French & German descent, and had changed his name from Shillingburg to Knight. He used to sit me on his lap, he had a huge tattoo on his chest of a galleon and he would breathe in and out to make it look as if the sails were billowing in the wind. When I looked at them, he would say in what he thought was a sailor's voice, "You and me are going on that boat one day to Calif-orn-ia."

To be honest, I can't ever remember him standing up, he was always sitting in a wooden rocking chair to the right of the fire. It wasn't a romantic fire like an Aga, but a functional one, and the fire was always on. On top of that fire there was always a kettle boiling, ready for a cup of tea. Tea was the thing. Everybody had a cup of tea when they came in. If you were well-off, you had carpet, but we had Lino. There was a small kitchen off the living room, and outside there was a yard where my grandad kept chickens in a coup. Everybody kept chickens in those days, if you had a backyard, because they'd be fattened up for Christmas lunch.

There was an outside toilet. I'd never ever seen an inside toilet; I didn't know they existed until much later in my life. It is hard to think now, that back then you had to go outside to have a pee! Never mind what the weather was like. There was no such thing as loo paper, although perhaps rich people had it? I spent a lot of time with my grandparents, and one of my jobs was to cut the newspapers up into bits and put them on a hook. And under the bed there was a pot, which we called a po, that was used to save them from going outside in the cold.

One day, I woke up at Fatty Nan's and the house next door was gone. That is how much we must have been used to the noise, because I didn't wake up in the night and it must have made such a racket. I went downstairs and saw that the chickens had been blown up. I went and told my grandad that his chickens had done a bunk. The girl next door, who used to be my play friend, was now dead. All I could see was her arm lying on the toilet roof. I remember it as vividly as anything. You got so used to death.

I loved my days in Camberwell. Mum was busy being an ambulance driver but still used to come and visit me at Fatty Nan's. I remember she once gave me five shillings to go into Camberwell High Street to run an errand. On the way there I passed a funfair, and the bright lights lured me in. Before I could say Jack Robinson I'd spent all the money on the rides, for which I got a good hiding when I got home.

I used to go to the cinema. There were two in Camberwell, one we nicknamed 'The Bug Hutch' because it was so run down, and there was a Variety Theatre as well. I used to bunk into all the cinemas, as I had no money. The men's toilets had a window that you could look out of when you were having a pee. Many a time, I'd climb through the window and men, while peeing, would pull me inside and tell me what a rascal I was for not paying the sixpence to get in. I'd often see horror films and be so frightened on the way back to Fatty Nan's I'd walk in the middle of the road in the dark, which somehow felt safer. As it happens, near Fatty Nan's house, just past the tuck shop, was a canal where a man used to put his willy through the fence, and if you pulled it, he'd give you sixpence.

When mum finished working as an ambulance driver, we moved to Croxted Road, which was the main road to Crystal Palace. School was in Dulwich. I remember walking past Dulwich Hamlet, wondering what it was. That was the posh school where I later found out the likes of Bob Monkhouse were educated. That was really a toff's school, that you probably had to pay for, but I was at an ordinary school.

I used to go to school with a gas mask under my arm. I'd walk there picking up shrapnel. Some of it was still hot as it had just fallen off planes from the sky. I'd get to school and swap the different shapes I'd found with the other boys.

School was a pretty awful place. The windows had been bricked up to stop a bomb blast, and the buildings were in a terrible state of decay. Every time an air-raid siren wailed into life we sat under our desks, or huddled into a cupboard or a dark room. In those days, you didn't go to school to learn anything, you went to school because that's what you had to do. So, I hated school and was no good at anything anyway. One of my earliest memories was the boys chasing the girls into the girls toilets. It wasn't a sexual thing, it was just something they did. Then, the girls would come to me and say, "So and so and so is chasing me into the toilets, and they won't stop." So, after school every day I'd have these fights with the boys. I was the best-looking boy in the school, and I was the best fighter in the school. So, my favourite part of the day was after school when we had these bundles.

On Fridays, mums used to pick us up. I was so thrilled when mum would come, because she was the most beautiful, and I'd see her on the other side of the railings with a lovely hat on, looking absolutely fantastic. My school teacher I called Fatty Arbuckle, after the famous actor. In those days, we all used to get the cane a lot, especially me. He used to pretend to drop his cufflinks, and say, "Pick them up, James," and then he'd give me a whack on the arse with his cane. You held your hands out, so your knuckles were up, and then he'd hit you with a ruler. And as he hit me, I could see the blood coming out of my knuckles. It was really awful that teachers were allowed to do that. I also used to stand in the corner with a dunce's hat on, and people used to look at me. I mean, people still look at me now, but I don't have the dunce's hat on!

So, I didn't like school at all. I was a loner. I was very happy with my own company. But if I wasn't on my own, I was the leader of the pack. Boys always wanted to be with me because I was the best fighter in the school and I always got up to mischief, so they always followed me. Wilson was my best friend, but one day he didn't show up to school, and when the teacher called out his name and he didn't answer I overheard the headmaster reply, "Air raid victim." My ears pricked up as I realised they thought Wilson had been killed in an air raid, which was a normal occurrence then. He hadn't. He just hadn't turned up for school. In those days, the mother would always write a note saying so and so isn't well and give it to the neighbour. So, I thought, that's an idea, if I don't come to school, they'll think I'm an air raid victim!

So, after that, I used to leave for school every day like clockwork. Mum used to give me my milk money, which was a halfpenny, and I'd be like Huckleberry Finn; I'd get on the bus to go to the West End. I'd go to Brockwell Park and become Robin Hood. I'd go up to Crystal Palace, which had just been burnt down, and there were big old statues. It was a wonderland. I'd buy a loaf with the halfpenny that mum gave me and eat bits of it through the day, leaving the crusts 'til last. I'd have a wonderful time and come back home at half past three when my mum would say, "Have a good day, Gerry Boy?" and I'd say, "Yes mum, I did." So that went on for about six months.

Until one day, the school board man came to my house and knocked on the door and said to my mother, "Mrs James, I'm sorry to hear of the demise of your boy." She said, "Demise? What do you mean demise?" She didn't know what the word meant. "Well," he said, "Your boy Gerald James hasn't been to school for six months." She said, "Of course he bleeding-well has, he goes to school every day. Now sling your hook!" So, off the school board man went, with his tail between his legs.

That day, I returned home at the normal time as I always did, went through the door and mum was waiting for me. She said to me, "Did you have a good day at school, Gerry Boy?" as she always did, and smilingly, I said, "Oh, yes mum."

"Did Fatty Arbuckle give you the cane again?" she asked.

"I'm afraid so mum, yes." I replied. Before I knew it, she turned to me and said, "You bleedin' toe rag. You ain't been to school for six months!"

"Yes, I have mum." I answered back. Then she told me that the school board man had been 'round and told her all about my larks. She always said that if I was naughty, she'd put me in the coal hole where the gingerbread boy lived. The coal hole was the door under the stairs. You opened the door and went down the steps, and under the house was where you kept the coal. The coal came from the coal man at the front of the house after he lifted up a round, iron lid. Why people didn't get burgled through the coal hole I don't know, but they never did. Mainly, I suppose, because the big iron lid was so heavy to lift up. Also, the inside door was always locked. So, as my punishment, mum put me under the stairs. It was dark, and I was shaking. I was so frightened. I thought the gingerbread boy was going to gobble me up. I was beside myself with fear. Finally, she let me out and said, "Now tomorrow you better get back to school, you little rascal!".

As there was no television in those days, the radio was the be-all and end-all. I used to sit on her lap and listen to a show called *The Man in Black* played by an actor called Valentine Dyall who had this really creepy voice and told horror stories. Many years later, when I made Agatha Christie's *The Body in the Library* in 1984 with Joan Hickson, I noticed that he was on the call sheet. I was so thrilled. It was like meeting Boris Karloff, who in reality was a really sweet, nice man. Valentine Dyall was the same, nothing like his image. Well, I guess none of us are like our image, are we? Although, I try!

I had so many jobs while I was at school. I was the Coal man's boy, which meant I'd sit next to the coal man on his horse and cart and help him by calling out when we arrived at people's houses, dropping the coal down the coal hole. Everybody had a coal hole in the front of their house. I doubled that job up with collecting horse manure, which I then sold on to housewives for gardening. I was also the milkman's boy and delivered the milk for him, which involved me emptying a great big milk churn into a jug that the customer brought out from the house as there were no milk bottles in those days. So, in the end, I was very glad to leave school because I got to earn a living. Plus, on Saturdays I'd earn an extra shilling by cleaning the windows for mum.

There were bombs dropping, and you could be killed any time. Yet, it was all part and parcel of the way we lived. You looked up into the sky and you heard the air-raid sirens going off that warned you that the bombers were on their way. I saw some bad things. I remember coming out of the cinema in Herne Hill having watched *They Died with Their Boots On* starring Errol Flynn, who was mine and my mum's favourite film star. As I left the cinema there was a double decker bus with the top blown off, full of dead passengers. I went home and told mum all about the film and not a mention of the horrors I'd seen on the bus. Seeing dead people was pretty much a daily occurrence in the war, whereas seeing Errol Flynn was something special. The magic of the cinema became my reality, rather than reality itself. Another time, a plane crashed with a German soldier in it, and the wives all went with pitchforks and apparently finished him off. That was the way it was then. One of things I'd do after a house got bombed, was go in there and bring things home to my mum; plates, saucers, all sorts of things. I did it because I thought it would make mum happy, and that she'd think I was a good boy by doing it.

The sleeping arrangements were strange during the war. They said it wasn't safe in the house because of the bombs dropping, so one of the things we used to do was sleep in the London Underground station. The underground for us, living in Brixton, was Stockwell. It wasn't until many years later that Brixton had its own tube station. At night, we would get a bus from Brixton to the Oval with a blanket and we'd sleep in the underground. We didn't like it there much. There were lots of people crammed in and it was pretty uncomfortable, and people sang all night. So that didn't last for long. Another way of sleeping was to sleep under a table at home, so if the house was bombed that would protect you. Or you'd sleep in the air raid shelter in the garden. They were awful little places, they looked like mud huts. You'd go in and there were two little bunk beds. I remember it being very damp. We slept in all these places, but if you had a direct hit you were going to be killed anyway.

The other thing I remember about the war is the fact that my mum had five brothers, and for some unknown reason they all finished up in the navy. They used to come home from leave and jump off the number 3 bus in their sailor's uniforms. In those days, anybody in a uniform was treated like God. I was so thrilled that they were my uncles, and the neighbours used to come out to see them and wave.

We lived on a railway line, and the Yanks used to come past on trains throwing chewing gum out, which was a big luxury then, because we had never heard of chewing gum until the Yanks arrived. They were known for giving housewives nylon stockings. They also introduced us to powdered milk. The powers that be sent all our men overseas. My father was in Iceland. God knows why he was there, as England was full of Yanks.

The Yanks were so handsome, as most of them came from sunny places so they were nice and dark and tanned. A lot of them were black, and I'd never seen black people before, except in the movies, like Louis Armstrong and the very handsome Harry Belafonte. I thought the American uniforms were so much more glamorous than ours. Their uniforms were sparkly and bright blue, and ours were dull and grey. Obviously, as all the women were alone, the Yanks used to take them out and date them. The Cumberland Hotel in Marble Arch was the big hangout for the Yanks and the foyer was always full of women, mostly housewives, dressed up to the nines, waiting to be chatted up. Of course, they could go for walks in Hyde Park with them. Lots of women ended up pregnant while their husbands were away fighting, and wrote letters saying, "I've given birth and he looks just like you?" I was very aware of all this, and I was only young at the time, although, I must say, I never ever saw my mother with a Yank.

# 2: Dad Returns from the War

My dad was pretty much a stranger to me when he finally came back from the war. The first thing he did was buy a greengrocer's shop in Herne Hill, which was adjacent to Brockwell Park, and which became my playpen where I would act out all the films I had seen. I'd be Errol Flynn as Robin Hood and play cowboys and Indians. Brockwell Park was such an exciting place, with the biggest lido in South London where, more often than not, you'd have to queue to get in. Locals would watch football every Sunday with crowds three-deep. The funfair came once or twice a year and was run by traditional gypsies. I became friendly with one of the gypsy boys and was fascinated to see that he had more fingers than me! Looking back, I realise how lucky people in that area were to have such a wonderful place to enjoy.

I became resentful of dad coming between me and mum as we were so close. Each day, she would do different things. Monday was always going to the flicks, with the traditional fish and chips on the way home; a structure I'd continue pretty much throughout my life. One day was laundry, the next day was tidying the house, the next was shopping, and at about four o'clock mum would get changed into a nice dress for the evening, as that was when dad finished work. Dad was a very clever man. We would move house all the time from place to place, as dad was a bit of a wheeler-dealer. He would always sell the house for more money than he paid for it. I remember when we lived in Brixton, we lived in a house with no wall. There was a tarpaulin up for years. Dad's mum, Granny James, lived next door. That was a happy time, in Brixton. I had the Brixton Empress, where I used to go and see the likes of Max Miller, Wee Georgie Wood, Old Mother Riley, a very young Max Bygraves, all the great stars. In those days you even had to queue to get into the gods for the six penny seats where we would always sit. I often wondered what it would be like to sit downstairs, nearer to the stage where you could see the acts up close.

Nearby, we had the Camberwell Palace and three cinemas in Brixton. There were cinemas everywhere and I was a great film fan. I'll never forget the atmosphere of walking home through the market. I had a feeling of well-being, and when I got home there was the traditional cockney cup of tea.

Friday night was bath night, and there was only ever enough water for one bath. Mum and dad were first in, and by the time I got in the water was lukewarm. Oh, what joy! We would play football every evening until it was dusk. I remember a neighbour coming and asking if her son could come and play football with Gerry Boy, as her son was such a wimp. So, boys wanted to be in my gang, and I was soon to find out that girls did too. At the age of twelve, I went to a party where I was seduced by a girl of sixteen. I realized then that there might be a bit more going on in life than kicking a ball up against a wall!

As a teenager I was angry, and I don't really know where my anger came from, but I was angry about something. I don't know if it was because I couldn't read or write, or the fact that when my father came back from war he kind of took mum away from me. Mum & I were very close, although

I think she would have preferred a daughter. When I was a teenager, I had a dressing table with a vanity mirror. Over the years people have always said to me, "Why have you got such good skin?" I don't know if it is genetic because mum's brothers, who were all in the Navy, all had baby-faces but I never shaved until I was fifteen. From an early age, mum used to tell me I had great cheekbones and that I should make sure I put Nivea on them, to accentuate them. Mum would allow me to bring girls home at night and sleep with them. She was so used to me bringing

*Me, at the age of twelve*

girls back, she'd come in in the morning and say, "Ooh, I've not seen this one before!"

Yet she was this ordinary sort of woman. She seemed to enjoy the fact that I had lots of girlfriends, it really didn't bother her at all. She almost brainwashed me into thinking, with my dark blue eyes and good looks, I would break a million hearts. It was almost like that became my destiny.

Around this time, with dad's wheeling and dealing, we were shuffled off to a place called Walton-on-Thames where dad had bought a nursery, because by this time he'd sold the greengrocer's shop and was the owner of *Clement Le Roy*, a flower shop in Shepherds Bush. I didn't want to go into the flower business, but I didn't know what I wanted to do. In those days, there was work everywhere and you could do what you wanted to. I wasn't sure what I wanted to do, but I wasn't keen on becoming a florist, as it didn't fit my Teddy Boy image.

So, I took a job as a stainless-steel vessel worker in Kingston. Dad used to drop me off on his way to Covent Garden Flower Market. I hated every minute of working in a factory. My job consisted of me being inside a steel vessel, while somebody on the other side hit it with a hammer. The only thing I could do to break the monotony was to go to the toilet as often as I could to smoke a cigarette, and I didn't even smoke! One day, my best mate there cut his finger off in the lathe. They said to me, "Gerry, take it, he's gone to the hospital." So I had to take his finger in an envelope on the bus to the hospital, and they gave me half a crown for the fare. But no sooner had I walked out the factory door, I thought I'd save the money and walk and do some window shopping. Kingston was a fabulous place for fashion and there were certain shops where you could get fashionable shirts and ties. After some time, deciding what I would look good in and buy on my next pay packet, I thought I'd better get this finger to the hospital. When I arrived, I handed over my best mate's black sausage of a finger! A week later my best mate returned to work sporting this black finger, and every time I saw him it reminded me of the fact that I had been a right bastard, not getting the finger to him quicker.

In the end, I couldn't stand another day in the factory and left because I thought anything must be better than being a factory worker, which I certainly wasn't cut out to be. Dad kept inviting me to work with him. I know the flower business, because I've been to the shop, and it's going to be an easy ride for me because I'll be the under-manager or whatever I'll be, but I'll certainly be the boss's son. He's also going to let me off Monday afternoons to go to the pictures with my mum. Funnily enough, that was the thing that sold it to me. He didn't actually give me Mondays off, but I stopped work soon after lunch in Shepherds Bush and got the tube to Waterloo then the train to Walton-on-Thames and met mum in the foyer of the cinema, every Monday which was a great joy. Mum would be sitting there looking lovely, having tea in the ABC cinema.

I thought to myself, if you're a florist, you've got to be a proper florist. So dad paid for me to go to Constance Spry in Knightsbridge to learn my trade. I was the only boy in the class, so I felt like a kid in a candy store with lots of sweets on offer, and I sampled most of them! I'd go there a couple of times a week and learn how to do flower arrangements and make wreaths, culminating in me getting my Constance Spry diploma in flower arranging. Getting this diploma was a great achievement, but it would come back to haunt me many years later when I became a star; famous comics would refer to it, as it wasn't very rock 'n' roll.

In those days, we drove from Hersham, which is Walton-on-Thames, into Covent Garden Flower Market every morning. I don't remember getting up that early, I'm not even sure it wasn't earlier than half past eight. Everybody knew dad, and he wanted me to watch him so he could teach me the business and be able to barter over the flowers. Then he would buy all these flowers, and his driver there, who had the Clement Le Roy van, would bring all the flowers back to the shop. We'd get back to the shop at about ten o'clock, and in the middle of Shepherds Bush green there was a place where taxi drivers used to have their breakfast called a Cabman's shelter, one of those little green huts. Even though we weren't cabbies, we'd go there for our breakfast, as dad was a local character. After breakfast, I'd dress the window, rearranging all the flowers and putting them on stands and making them attractive. I'd take orders for weddings and make the bouquets and wreaths. Every lunchtime, I'd go to Bertorellis and have a big lunch. The Bertorellis became family friends, and years later when I went to Majorca, they'd all retired there, and invited me to perform cabaret in their big restaurants.

I was always in the shop. Women used to come in and say they'd only want to be served by me. Before long, dad gave me my own shop, which was opposite the Shepherds Bush Empire. Behind Shepherds Bush Empire was, of course, Gainsborough Studios. Being so close to the studios, a lot of the actors used to come in on their way home to buy flowers for their mums or girlfriends. So, I met lots of actors then. At the start of every Gainsborough Studios Film, you'll see an elegant woman nodding, wearing a very exotic headdress. I'm proud to say I made that, an image that has become iconic and is still being shown today.

*The Gainsborough Studios Logo*

By this time, the most important thing in my life was the opposite sex. Equally important was being a Teddy Boy. Saturdays, our gang would walk up and down Walton-on-Thames High Street. You couldn't afford a drape or jeans, because jeans came from America, and you couldn't get them. So we used to have boiler suits, the sort that workmen used to work in. We'd cut the tops off and put a belt on, so we had the jean-type bottoms. I used to wear my dad's jacket, which was two sizes too big, which made it look like a drape and I'd walk around Woolworths looking for birds. My life then was taking dates to the cinema, never watching the film but being fully concentrated on having a snog, slowly moving one arm around their shoulders while the other would tickle their knee and then bullseye!

As a Teddy Boy, I was up to no good. A good night out was a knee-trembler, or having a bundle. They were both equal to me. It was either having sex, which happened almost every night I went out, or if I didn't have sex, I would have a fight with someone. I liked fighting, and I knew how to look after myself. I always carried a knife, and would threaten people. I'd fix it onto where my braces were and I would pull it out and say, "Fuck off, otherwise I'll cut ya!" That kind of bunny.[1] Nowadays, they stab people and kill them. In my day, it was more of a theatrical threat.

Back then, it was the 'in' thing to have been cut and have a shiv mark on your face, that was like a mark of honour if you had a slash on your face. Truthfully, I looked at myself in the mirror so many times, with a razor blade in one hand, and been so close to cutting myself to complete the full gangster look, but I think vanity or being squeamish about cutting myself stopped me.

In those days, Hollywood seemed to glamorise gangsters, and all teenage boys wanted to be like them. So here I was, nicking lead off roofs, which I could then sell. I remember even getting myself into a few scrapes with the police. I remember once, police cars came, and I was running and running and running, and I jumped over this wall and knocked myself unconscious. I was lying there on the other side of the wall, thinking the police are gonna get me now, and they never did. Looking back, I didn't need money, I didn't want to hurt anybody, but it was a fantasy. I wanted to play out scenes I'd seen in films, as strange as that may seem. If only I'd known that I could be a gangster, as an actor on screen, and get paid for it, which I did very successfully years later.

In the midst of all this, my mother heard from a neighbour that they were looking for somebody to work backstage at the local amateur theatre company. At that time, I wasn't interested in going on stage, in my mind that was for posh people, but mum liked the idea and she made me go. I would operate the spotlight and shine it onto these actors. I thought it was all wonderful, and I followed these amateur actors around backstage. A lot of them didn't speak to me very much and seemed stuck up, maybe it was because I didn't speak as posh as them, but I knew I looked as good, perhaps even better than them, and before long I felt I had a connection with this acting lark. People laugh at me, but being as good looking as I am, it is a burden in many ways. People think it's wonderful, but it isn't. You have a lot to live up to. I mean, it's no good being a good-looking boy and being a bus driver. If you're a good-looking boy, the thing to be is in showbusiness. So that's how, I suppose mentally, I found my way into the right business to be in. I didn't want to make wreaths and crosses for dead people all my life, did I?

---

1. Bunny = Talk, from cockney rhyming slang (bunny) rabbit & pork

*Teddy Boy Jess and a friend*

# 3: West End Boy

I went to Soho. I was fascinated by it all, and it wasn't long before I was rubbing shoulders with the underworld. The life of crime seemed glamorous. Gangsters were very striking characters, just like they were in the movies, charismatic and compelling. The Krays, The Richardsons, Jack Spot, even as villains they had great sense of humour amongst themselves, and I would often see them helping old ladies across the road. To become one of them and join their ranks seemed like a very attractive proposition to me.

I first saw the Kray Twins in a newspaper article with a glamorous peroxide blonde on their arm. I'd never seen a blonde British woman before, women with blonde hair had all been Hollywood sex symbols. I later realized, when we became friends, that the peroxide blonde was a young Barbara Windsor. The Krays were star-struck and wanted to be associated with sexy women, so it was a feather in their cap to act on behalf of stars like Diana Dors and Barbara Windsor, if men were showing them unwanted attention. If anyone took a liberty with them, because they knew the Krays, the bloke would be seen to. If Dors said she was having trouble with a man, they would sort him out. Back then, the gangsters had great morality. They would never swear in front of wives or girlfriends, they were very respectful of their mothers because of the role they had played during the war. You never pinched another man's wife or mistress, there was a strict code of honour. There was a Robin Hood thing about them, that they only got involved with other gangsters.

The place to go was Sissy Jackson's, just behind the Windmill Theatre in Soho, where gangsters like The Krays were often seen. Now remember, back then I didn't know anyone in showbusiness, so hanging out with the likes of The Krays seemed glamorous. When they walked in it was like a film star had walked in. Many men, including myself, were in awe of the gangsters and the way they dressed and carried themselves, and we were attracted to them. You have to remember this was a time after the horror of the war and London had been left in an awful state. The only glamour was on the cinema screen, and that was people who played gangsters like James Cagney & Edward G Robinson. They glorified the life of crime.

But there was a darker side. Ronnie Kray was a predatory homosexual who terrified young men in Soho in the 1960s. I remember the barman would warn you to make yourself scarce 'cos The Krays were on their way! Good looking young men used to vanish for fear of catching Ronnie's eye and being invited back to their place. It was like an invite you couldn't turn down. You had to keep your wits about you.

It was only when I became involved with screen siren Dors, who mixed with tough guys, that I met the Krays and went to parties they were at. Once I started to be successful in showbusiness and became friends with other stars, I saw them more regularly. They would come to Dors' parties at her house and behave like perfect gentlemen.

I spent most of my time in some of the outrageous nightclubs in Soho where I was often picked up by older women, who were invariably on the game, or chased by homosexual men. I was wined and dined in all the elegant West End Clubs by glamorous ladies and famous men, and I played both sexes along for my own ends. It was like being in a film. It was very fashionable to go tea dancing. I'd often find rich women whose husbands had died or they'd divorced, or they were just randy women of a certain age, and I'd start relationships with whoever I wanted to. The richer, the better. Attractiveness didn't come much into it. I always liked to be the attractive one! There were lots of situations where I was in Soho and I was dancing with these women. They were looking after me, they were feeding me, I was half living with them. Then, I met this one that turned out to be a prostitute, and she wanted to look after me. The first time I met her, I was in her flat and I went into the bathroom, and there was a man bollock-naked on the toilet, tied up with a handkerchief around his face. He was like, gagged, and he was making these terrible noises. I said, "What's the matter?" as he was in such distress. So, I undid the handkerchief then he jumped up and ran out. My friend came back and said, "Where's Claude?"

"Who's Claude?" I said. "There was a man in the toilet crying…"

She said, "You silly fucker, that was a customer! He likes being tied up! Fuck me, you've got a lot to learn!"

When I reached eighteen, I was eligible for national service, if only they could find me. The army kept serving me with call-up papers, but I kept deferring them. I wasn't going into the army if I could help it, and that was final. I would rather have done a prison sentence! The West End was so good for me, and my life was absolutely fantastic. However, eventually, they did catch up with me and I was summoned to Catford for my army medical, but I still tried all the tricks to avoid going in.

Somebody said, "If you swallow a bar of soap, your heart will beat irregularly". So, I swallowed a bar of soap and went into a coma and got rushed to hospital. So, that didn't work. Reluctantly, after a few weeks, I reported for duty, resigned to my fate yet still thinking, "What am I going to do now?"

On the day, I arrived at this funny little place in Catford together with a host of other would-be soldiers, all very ordinary blokes, which I'd never considered myself to be. By now, I'd become a smart West End animal. Suave, sophisticated, and worldly, or so I thought. To see these dowdy guys, all my own age, queuing up for their medicals was a definite culture shock for me. To add insult to injury, the first thing we were asked to do on arrival was to strip down to our underwear. I soon noticed everyone was looking at me, staring at my underpants. In those days, there was only one kind of underwear available on the market, baggy white underpants. These were the days long before boxer shorts or briefs, or any kind of sophisticated underwear. However, as one of the West End set, I had my own underpants especially made for me off Carnaby Street, long before it became famous as the centre of fashion, at a men's boutique called *Vince*. Vince used to make briefs for all the chaps in the know. They were basically like skin-hugging swimming trunks, and he turned them out in a variety of colours. So, my underpants were the centre of attention and caused quite a stir amongst the other would-be soldiers, which gave me an idea, "Oh Gerry boy, I think I'll pretend to be bent! There's just a chance it might work."

The 1950s was a very dour period for male fashions and very few men wore jewellery. Although, I was very partial to wearing rings and medallions without thinking. So apart from my underwear, I was also wearing a couple of rings on my fingers and a large medallion around my neck, which I've always worn. I was standing there stripped to the waist, in my briefs and wearing my jewellery, and was becoming a talking point among the other recruits until at last I was summoned to see the chief medical officer. I walked into his office and dropped my shorts. No sooner had I done so, I got an erection! So, I reached for the first thing I could find, the officer's peak cap which was hanging on a hat stand next to me, and covered my embarrassment. As I sat down, it looked as if a dwarf was sitting on my lap wearing a military cap and peeping over the top of the desk!

"What do you think you're doing with my cap?" the officer barked. Then, in a much softer voice he said, "Do you mind if I ask you a personal question?"

"That depends on what it is", I replied.

"Well," he continued, "where did you get that jewellery you're wearing?"

"That's my business," I replied, before continuing, "Actually, it was a present from a *friend*."

After a beat, he continued, "Hmmm. Was this friend male or female?"

It was then I thought I'll play the gay card and I replied, "I really don't have to answer this," and I was now very slowly breaking into this very camp voice and getting quite emotional. "In fact, it was from a man." I said. There was a long silence before he proceeded to ask me a series of academic questions to see how intelligent I was.

He thought for a moment and then asked, "Who robbed the rich and gave to the poor and lived in Sherwood Forest? Having had little or no formal education through my lack of schooling, I genuinely didn't know the answer, so I said, "Sinbad the sailor." He looked at me in complete and utter amazement. I explained that I'd seen Sabu playing him in the film. By this time, the officer was losing his cool. I told him I'd seen a great movie at the Golden Domes cinema in Camberwell with a genie in a bottle. By now he was totally confused and didn't know what to make of this idiot standing in front of him with a hard-on talking about Sabu!

He tried another question and asked, "Who was shot in the eye at the battle of Hastings?" to which I replied, "I don't know, sir. I haven't seen that film yet!" He was getting progressively more distraught the longer the interview went on, and before long I realized that he was probably gay himself and trying to hide that fact.

Before ending the interview, he asked me one final question, "What do you do for a living?" I replied, "I'm a male model."

"And what do you model?"

"Swimsuits sir, because everything looks good." He'd had enough, and dismissed me immediately. I left the room, and to complete my performance, I minced across the floor and out of the door. Every head turned towards me. Just as I was leaving the building, the officer called me back to collect my underpants that I'd left in the middle of the floor.

A few days later, I received a letter telling me I was unsuitable for national service and added that if I wanted to know why I had been turned down I should get in touch with my local doctor. I wasn't bothered about that, I'd managed to escape the clutches of Her Majesty's services and I was back in the West End with far more important things to do, like having a good time. The fact that I was off the hook was enough.

Around this time, I met a girl called Gloria, who was also a Pisces and born the same date as me. So, that was probably the connection. Gloria lived in a building in Stamford Hill, and I used to climb in her window and stay the night. Her dad used to knock on the door and say, "Good night." I used to get up about five or six o'clock in the morning and creep out. Eventually, Gloria fell pregnant and her family, who were strict Jews, would never let their daughter marry a Christian boy. So, to break up our relationship they packed her off to her relatives in America. I was broken-hearted. Our daughter was taken away and given to somebody in America. That must have broken Gloria's heart. Gloria was my big love and God knows how it would have turned out, but I would have married her, and we could have been happy. It wasn't until 2021 that my long-lost daughter Marianne got in touch with me. It was a tremendous shock to know that my daughter actually existed. Through sheer determination, she had found out who her mother and father were. I was thrilled to hear from her, and coincidentally she is an actress living in Hollywood. Who knows, perhaps one day she'll come to visit? Or vice versa.

When Gloria left, I continued to be a West End face. After a busy night, to wind down, I used to walk down Piccadilly towards Park Lane, where there was a very popular coffee shop, as I'd seen Maxwell Reed do it once.

*The Legrain Coffee House in Gerrard Street*

He was the biggest film star in England, the closest thing we had to Victor Mature; one of our biggest heartthrobs. That's how I started the habit of walking down there.

One night, having finished my coffee and wondering what to do next, I was standing out by the curb, having a pose-up, and a Roller pulled up. The driver wound down the window and said to me, "The lady in the back would like to have a word with you." Sitting there in the back seat, appeared to be an aging Ava Gardner. Then, when she spoke, I realised it was the *actual* Ava Gardner! She asked me if I'd like to come back for a coffee, and I said yes. It seems like if you're the right person, in the right place, at the right time, the strangest things can happen.

It was around this time that I became friends with Kenny Lynch. We used to go to the same jazz clubs. He was the smartest guy you've ever seen. The crease on his trousers you could cut your finger with, as he was so sharp. I'd often go with him to see his sister Maxine Daniels, who used to sing at the Lyceum. Then we'd go into the Harmony Inn Cafe around the corner from the Windmill Theatre. Then, something happened that changed my life forever...

I'd just been into the cinema and seen *Caesar and Cleopatra*. I was sitting having my milk and a dash in Legrain. At the time, I didn't really know it was an actor's hangout, yet I found myself in it. Lots of the guys there were model-types, the likes of Michael Caine and Terence Stamp, long before they were famous. All of a sudden, a fella walked in and as there was a space at my table, he sat down opposite me. He had a very distinctive face, a handsome man with a beard. I said, "Hang on a minute, I've just seen you in a movie"

"That's right," he said proudly, "I'm an actor." His name was Larry Taylor, and he played the third centurion from the left. So, he wasn't a major star, it was just the fact that I just come out of the cinema where I'd seen this film and one of the actors was right there in front of me. So, I asked him, "How do you get into the film business?"

He looked at me and said, "Well, you're good-looking, kid."

I said, "Well there's nothing wrong with your eyesight!" and we both laughed. He went on to explain that next to The Palladium is the FAA; Film Artists Association, run by a woman, and that if I went around there, I might be able to charm her into becoming a film extra. So, without hesitation, I go around there, and explain that I have just met Larry Taylor. The woman said, "Oh, we all know Larry." Then she went on to ask, "Do you have a good wardrobe?" Puzzled, I asked, "What do you mean?"

"Well," she said, "Do you have a swimsuit?" Unimaginable these days to ask somebody something like that as everybody has a swimsuit! But, in those days they didn't. So it went on. "Do you have black trousers?"

"Yes."

"Do you have a tweed jacket?"

"Yes."

"Do you have a black jacket?"

"Yes."

And then came the killer question, "Do you have a dinner jacket...?" which usually meant if you didn't have one, you'd be out of the door. She was poised for the usual answer of "No" when I surprised her by saying, "Oh, yes." She was taken aback. I said, "Yes, my father is a Mason and every year they have the ball for the wives. So, my dad bought me a dinner jacket when I was about fourteen or fifteen." At which point she looked at me and smiled broadly as if to say, "Welcome to the film industry." I drove home on cloud nine in my Hillman Minx, and that night I had a phone call from the FAA to report at Pinewood Studios at 8:30 in the morning.

# 4: Film Extra

I woke up the next morning full of bonhomie for the day that lay ahead. By this time, my parents had moved to Dulwich, to a house called Jerrylynn, which was half my dad's name and half my mum's. Today, it would probably take three hours to drive from Dulwich to Pinewood, but I certainly didn't get up that early. I drove over Lambeth Bridge, past the Houses of Parliament, around Piccadilly Circus, down to Marble Arch, and then up the A40 to Pinewood. When I went through the famous Pinewood Gates, I felt like I was entering wonderland.

My first job as an extra was in *Cockleshell Heroes* in 1955, a war film directed by José Ferrer. Next, I worked on *Joe MacBeth*, an American crime drama loosely based on Shakespeare's *Macbeth*. It was my hand holding an umbrella, and for that I got paid £2/10d a day. With my good looks and a good wardrobe, I got my fair share of extra work.

Soon, I was given my first small part, and when the film reached my local cinema my whole family turned up in force to see their boy. But my first real break came in 1956 when I was working on a film called *My Teenage Daughter,* which was intended to be a British *Rebel Without a Cause* and starred Anna Neagle and Sylvia Sims. The story concerned a mother who tries to deal with her teenage daughter's descent into delinquency. I disagreed with the sort of things the teenagers were being made to say, so I spoke up and told the director Herbert Wilcox, "This is not how teenagers talk!" It must have resonated with him, as I was then made the dialogue coach. Also, I was a good dancer, I used to win jiving competitions, so he brought me out of the crowd to do a jive and gave me a small part; one of the dancers in a jiving sequence.

On one occasion, I reported to the 3rd assistant director who checked my name and sent me to wardrobe, where I was decked out as a squaddie. I couldn't believe it, it was my first day on what I then discovered was *Reach for the Sky*, directed by Lewis Gilbert, and I was rubbing shoulders with the one and only Kenneth More, one of our most endearing film stars, who actually said, "Good morning" to me. I must have looked like an archetypal squaddie, as I seemed to go all the way through the film and even had a couple of close ups. We were taught how to march properly. On one occasion, they were setting up a prisoner of war scene where they needed close ups of squaddies that looked emaciated and malnourished for which I was chosen, as I was slim. Another extra stepped in line and was promptly told he was too fat. As quick as a flash, he said, "Yes guv'nor, but I was only captured yesterday!" That was the first indication I had of the things people would say or do to get what was then called Special Action.

The FAA union was very strong, and if we worked over a certain time we would get extra money. One time, I recall the 3rd assistant came looking for us fifteen minutes before the bell was about to ring, signifying the end of the day, and we were hiding in a cupboard. We could hear him saying, "Come on, last shot. Where are you?" Eventually the bell rang, and we went to pick up our money. The third assistant informed us that we would indeed be called the next day to finish off the shot we should have done that day. They knew what we were doing, but that was all part and parcel of the film extra game.

This was the first and most important change of direction in my entire life. I never looked back on my life of pretending to be a gangster. With a little luck and a lot of charm, I was now in the world of movies; the silver screen. Thus began one of the happiest phases of my whole career. As a film extra, I was working every day. I had people like Dirk Bogarde giving me the eye. I thought to myself, here we go again, some things never change.

Film extras didn't go in the stars' restaurant, as it was more expensive, but I ended up in there, because I was always invited. Whenever I went in the stars' restaurant, because the girl on the phone at the front desk at Pinewood studios had a crush on me, I would ask her to say my name over the Tannoy so all eyes would be on me. There were no mobile phones then! "Calling Gerry James…"

In those days, a lot of film stars had a special walk. John Wayne had a famous swagger. Although he was 6ft 2, he moved with great ease like a ballet dancer. Henry Fonda kind of leaned forward when he walked, he had a nice sort of flow. Robert Mitchum rolled from side to side, like a Teddy Boy's walk. So, as I was tannoyed, I tried out my special walk as I was called out of the main restaurant, thinking they would all take notice of me. As it happened, nobody took a blind bit of notice!

I felt I could talk to anybody I liked, even though I was only a film extra. Because of my experience with women, and the fact that I've always liked older women, I used to speak to the leading ladies. They were often Americans who were usually at the end of their career, a bit past their sell-by date, and making a film in England was their swansong. I would go over and say, "I hope you don't mind me saying, you were wonderful in that last scene." When you are a good-looking boy, it doesn't matter what you're saying because women seemed to be mesmerised by my looks and personality. They would often tell me that they had seen me earlier on and wondered who I was. Then, of course, I used to do the push and say, "Where are you staying?" They would answer, "In the Hilton Hotel," and before I knew it, they would invite me for dinner that night. I was wined and dined by stars like Ruth Roman, Yvonne DeCarlo, Linda Christian, and Gloria Grahame.

I once made love to the legendary Jayne Mansfield. We were in bed together about midnight when the phone rang. She picked up the receiver and found to her horror that it was her then husband, Mickey Hargitay. He was calling from America in the middle of the afternoon, sat by the pool in the glorious sunshine. As cool as ice, Jayne proceeded to talk to him as though I wasn't there. The perfect gentleman as always, I offered to call a halt to the proceedings while she finished her call. But she was having none of it, and begged me to carry on. After having made love to one of the most glamorous women in the world, while I was preening myself in front of the mirror she said, putting me in my place, "You do realise my husband was Mr Universe?!"

I had many clandestine liaisons with famous women, and many larks with gay men, but one of the most telling encounters was with Penny Dane, not her real name, who was a hostess at the Astor Club in Mayfair, one of London's most notorious nightspots, and she was also a film extra. She took a fancy to me and wouldn't take no for an answer. Having slept with her once, she insisted that I see her again. When I didn't wish to continue, she would suggest that if I would come around that evening, she'd have a very expensive gift for me. It would be something like gold chains or watches. This sort of relationship went on until I had no other space on my body for gold rings, medallions, or bracelets! I finally did break off the relationship, which was easier said than done.

I was an extra for about a year and worked with big stars like Arlene Dahl in *Wicked as they Come,* and *The Cockleshell Heroes* with José Ferrer. I was always on the set, you know, picking up crumbs, seeing what else I could do. Before long, I became a professional stand-in. I would stand for at least forty-five minutes before the shot, and they would make sure I was lit properly, then the star would come in and stand exactly where I had been. Several leading Hollywood actors came over from the states to film in Britain, many of whom I could tell were gay, although their publicity hand-outs said otherwise and labelled them all as macho men, famed for their powers with women. It simply was not true. I was frequently propositioned by some of the biggest stars in the movies. Clifton Webb, at the time, was a big American star, Oscar-nominated three times for his starring roles in *Laura*, *The Razor's Edge* and *Sitting Pretty*. When he saw me in the crowd he said, "I'd like that young man as my stand-in." I looked nothing like him!

Frankie Howerd was another. He became very friendly with me, and at the time used me in all the films he made. I would, more often than not, pick him up in my car, take him to the studio, and sit with him in his dressing room until he was called; because once you're a stand-in you're only called when the star is called, or to stand-in while they were lit. The third assistant was told where I could be found. One time, after a very boozy lunch, we went back to Frankie's dressing room and he dropped his trousers. I had never seen him behave like that before. I was upset and disappointed in him because I felt what I thought was a close matey friendship, although I knew he was gay, had turned into something else. I said to him in no uncertain terms, doing my best gangster impression, that if he didn't put his trousers back on that I'd cut both his fucking ears off, which frightened him to death. He hastily reassembled himself and never behaved inappropriately again with me.

As a stand-in, I would earn extra money and of course these famous actors got to know me as well. So, I soon realized it was a bonus to be 6ft 2 and attractive. When I went onto the set, directors used to ask, "Who's that?" and they'd give me extra bits to do.

I was an extra making a film with Alan Ladd who was a big Hollywood star, we all remember seeing him in *Shane*, but he was also famous for what they then called the Alan Ladd mac. All the West End boys wore a brown mac with the belt always tied in a knot, collar turned up was also essential. But, like most stars, he was a dwarf. I mean, tiny. He had lifts on his shoes. That was the first time I had ever seen them. They had to dig holes for his leading ladies to stand in, and he would stand on boxes. One day, the third assistant director who had become a mate said, "How would you like to have lunch with Alan Ladd?" When I got there Alan Ladd was sitting on this chair, which elevated him somehow. It looked as if he may have had it specially built for him by the props department. He certainly looked a lot taller. Everybody was pandering to him. They asked, "What kind of morning did you have, Al?" and he replied, "Well I had a great morning. I did a great look." Now, if you had said the same to Lawrence Olivier he would have said, "Darling boy, I did twelve pages without drying once. I knew every Dickie Bird."[2] But because this is a Hollywood actor, he talked about this great look, because he couldn't really act. That hit home to me. I thought to myself, fancy being in a position where you can just say, "I did a great look." and everybody applauds. Then I remembered the look he gave in *Shane*, when Shane's gone, and it became iconic in film history. Probably the best thing he had ever done!

Victor Mature was one of the biggest stars in Hollywood at the time. He was an enormous superstar and beefcake actor, famous for starring in the likes of *Samson & Delilah*, *The Robe* and *Demetrius & the Gladiators*. Like me, he loved women so we got on well. We were appearing together in a movie called *The Bandit of Zhobe* for Warwick Films. Victor Mature was the star, as an extra I was playing the part of a dervish. One morning we were all waiting for the star to arrive. He was late, of course. A friend of mine called Charlie Price acted as his double and stand-in. In actual fact, he was the real star of the film because Victor Mature would only come on the lot to film close-ups or two-shots and that was all. The rest of the scenes he left to his double Charlie. If there was a shot with three people in it, he would say, "Let Charlie do it," and he was off. Charlie did most of the work, horse riding, fighting, stunts. Yet despite that, Victor Mature was very charismatic. Wonderful. A real star, and he knew it.

We were shooting a dramatic scene inside a tent, in the desert, a big scene where Anne Aubrey was about to be burned to death by hostile dervishes, of which I was one. When he finally arrived on the set, the director took him to one side and said, "This is the pinnacle of the whole movie. We see that despite everything you do, you love your wife. This is the scene where the dervishes are going to burn your wife to death. It is an immensely powerful and dramatic moment. When I call action, I want you to come into the tent and see your wife burning. Victor, this is very important, not only for me but for you. We want this film to be a great success. We want you to be a great success in it. This is Oscar time. So, I really want you to emote."

Victor looked at the director and smiled, and said, "I tell you what I'll do. I will come into this tent. I can walk in slow or fast." He talked like it was a big deal and continued, "I have two speeds of walking and you can choose which one you like. Then, I can look at my wife and give her a three-quarter

---

2. Dickie Bird = Word

26

profile. I can smile, or I can keep a straight face and, just because I like you, I can make one eyebrow go up or down. Now, which of these looks would you like?" Victor Mature was someone you would never forget.

It was around that time an actor came onto set and had his name on the chair. He did two or three lines and had his own chair! I said, "I can do that," and they said, "No, that's a different union. That is Equity."

I said, "Well, how do you get into Equity?"

They said, "Well, you have to get an Equity card."

So, I said, "How do you get an Equity card?" And they said I would have to go into rep, as that's what you did in those days. Today, you don't even have to have an Equity card; Maggie Thatcher put an end to all that by getting rid of our union. But then, I thought to myself, this is a big crossroads for me. I can stay as I am, having a wonderful time, earning more money than I had ever seen and having lots of fun. Or, I could go into rep, where I would only earn in a week what I got in a day as a film extra. That is why a lot of good-looking boys like myself stayed as film extras, because the money was good, and they didn't have to take the risk of being an actor in another union and potentially being out of work. As I had changed my life from being a bit of a tearaway to an extra, I was determined to take the next leap from becoming an extra to an actor.

The last film I appeared in as a film extra was *Serious Charge* in 1959, directed by Terrence Young who went on to make three Bond films. The film starred Anthony Quayle, Andrew Ray and Sarah Churchill, who was Winston Churchill's daughter. I was already friendly with Andrew Ray who was the famous comedian Ted Ray's son. He became one of my closest friends after we met at one of Diana Dors's parties, which we will come to later. Andrew Ray played the leader of a gang of Teddy Boys who terrorized a town, which we filmed in Stevenage. The gang also included me and a young Cliff Richard. Cliff played a character called Curly, which meant that he was always in an hour before the rest of us, to have his hair curled, which he never seemed to mind, although there was actually no reason for his character to be called Curly. In one scene, Cliff sang his latest song *Living Doll* which went on to become a number 1 hit record. Through the making of this film Cliff & I became good friends and continue to be to this day. One day, Tommy Steele visited the set, who I also knew very well because, like Andrew Ray, he played for the Showbiz XI charity football team. Tommy met Cliff for the first time and there was an obvious rivalry.

In the pop world, Cliff was arguably a bigger star at the time, but he was very naïve. Tommy talked him into a game of knuckles. The object of the game was who could hit one another's knuckles the quickest and hardest. Tommy appeared to be master at this and had obviously played it many times before, while Cliff didn't really seem to understand the ferocity needed to win. Within a very short period of time, Cliff's knuckles were covered in blood, which shocked me. It seemed that Tommy was taking it out on Cliff because of his popularity.

At the end of the film, Andrew Ray had to do a dance, but he had no rhythm. So, I had to lie on the floor and move his legs, so it looked as though he was dancing. That scene had a dramatic climax when Anthony Quayle, who played the vicar and was running the youth club, was confronted by our gang of Teddy Boys, who came in and terrorized it. It was the final rehearsal before the take, and I realized this was my time to shine. I was looking menacing, with a bicycle chain wrapped around my wrist and Anthony Quayle turned to the director and said, obviously impressed with what I was doing, "Who is this guy?" Well, they were soon to find out, because I had decided that my next move would be to go into Repertory, learn my trade, get my Equity card, and become a bona fide actor.

# 5: Learning My Trade in Repertory

So, I go back to Legrain where it all started. Actors seemed to hang out there. I ordered my usual milk and a dash which was coffee in a tall glass with milk. Nothing exotic, but that is what we all drank then. It seemed the first thing to do was get a portfolio. This was a book-type thing with all your pictures in, showcasing yourself playing different parts. Well, I hadn't played any parts, only walk-ons as a film extra. So, I went to a photographer who said that I would make a fortune as a male model. I said, "No, I want to be an actor." He said, "Well, you've got to start somewhere." So, I went to see an agent called Pat Larthe. In her office, she had a picture of Roger Moore modelling knitwear and she told me I looked like him, and took me on. I thought if it was good enough for Roger Moore, it was good enough for me. So, I drifted into modelling and was making a good living, but I thought to myself I wouldn't get my Equity card that way.

So, I went to see another agent, who was also an actor, called John Penrose, because Pat Larthe told me he was the one who could get me into Rep. He said to me, "I think with my help you could make a good leading man. Show me your profile." Because, by that time, I had done so much modelling, I knew what to do. I turned one way to give him my left profile and the other to give him my right, and then looked straight-on and I noticed he was playing with himself under the desk!

I thought to myself, here we go again... but true to his word, he got me into rep.

The first rep I went to was Hornchurch. I could drive there from my house. I remember I had a red MG, as I was doing quite well as a model. In those days, showbusiness was a very glamorous industry. Even out of work actors dressed smartly; actresses always had an umbrella and wore black gloves, and actors rehearsed in suits and ties. One of my first jobs was playing one of the sailors in *Moby Dick*. I also did my first pantomime there and loved it. Then, I was very fortunate to be invited to become a member of the Charles Denville Repertory Company.

*The Charles Denville Repertory Company*

We were booked to do a season in Barnsley, Yorkshire, which was followed by a summer season in Aberystwyth in Wales. Charles Denville was one of the so-called great theatrical characters, complete with Homburg hat, dandruff on his collar and a wife called Lily who was sixty, if she was a day. He insisted on her playing the lead, no matter what the production was or how old the character she was portraying was supposed to be!

I joined the company at seven pounds ten shillings a week. Still, at least it gave me my Equity Card, and I certainly learned my trade. I was to be the ASM, assistant stage manager, which meant that I worked behind the scenes and got to play the small acting parts on stage. As ASM, I had to be in the theatre by ten a.m. to sweep and clean the stage and check the props so everything was hunky dory for the evening performance. One of my jobs was to get the props that the theatre didn't already have for all the different productions. One time, I had to get a four-poster bed. The pretty young housewife who I was getting it from insisted I try it out with her before taking it back to the theatre. Perks of the job! After a short time, I became quite well-known in the town, and had a thriving following of women fans who would come to the theatre hoping to see me and give me anything I asked for. We had more offers of props than we could ever use. Mostly beds!

Aberystwyth was a truly lovely seaside resort, and I was loving every moment of it. The first thing any actor must do is to find digs. By this time, I had fallen for one of the actresses, Billie Hammerberg, who had come over from Australia, as everybody did in those days, to make a name for herself in England. Nowadays, we all go to Australia where they now have a thriving

Entertainment industry, but not then. I suggested she change Hammerberg to a more poster-friendly name and came up with Laura Carl. Although she wasn't beautiful in the Scarlett O'Hara / Vivien Leigh sense, she had a great personality and was a very fine actress, more in the mode of Bette Davis. We had so much in common, with our love of acting and cinema. As we were part of the theatre, the two cinemas in Aberystwyth gave us complimentary tickets. We would sit in the cinema until five minutes before the half, which in layman's terms means half an hour before curtain-up. As the ASM, I had to call it. Then, we would rush from the cinema to the theatre. Later, when our show was finished, we would high-tail it back to the cinema and somehow catch the same film at the next showing at exactly the same point that we'd left off, more or less. Very rarely had we missed anything. Billie told me that she had found a lovely flat at the end of the promenade where the harbour was, so that is where we lived happily until the end of the season. On a Sunday, our only day off, we would go to the pub. She liked to drink, as most Australians seemed to, and watch television, which was a big thrill in those days. TV in those days was a small box in the corner of the room which everybody huddled around smoking and drinking.

The first part I played for Charles Denville in Aberystwyth was an elderly character who was supposed to be about sixty. He was married to a much younger woman played, of course, by the producer's wife Lily Denville. In reality, I was just twenty and Lily, who was meant to be younger than me, was forty years older than me! The first major problem I faced with the role was how to make myself up to look that old. One of the ways rep actors aged themselves in those days was to put Johnson's Baby Powder into their hair to whiten it and plaster their faces with grey looking makeup. So, I did that. But I was terrified. There I was, my first appearance on stage for Charles Denville, playing the part of a sixty-year-old man opposite the actor manager's wife, Lily Denville, who was a tyrant.

Come the performance that evening, we both made our entrances on cue, and as she walked in, she stopped and everybody applauded. I had no idea that she was going to stop. Of course, I know these things I know now, because I do them myself; you walk in, and you wait for the applause before you begin talking. Sometimes, I have seen actors wait an awful long time for the applause to start. Sometimes it never does start! But, back then, I didn't know that it was almost part of the tradition that they clapped Lily Denville, because she was the producer's wife. So, as she walked on and stopped, I kept walking and killed the applause. I also tripped over a chair leg and had to put my two hands out to stop me falling face-first onto the floor. I was scrambling about on all fours and the audience burst into spontaneous laughter and applause, obviously thinking it was part of the play. When I looked up, I saw a huge cloud of talcum powder hovering above my head like a snow-white halo! It just seemed to hang in the air.

The next morning, I was summoned in to see Charles Denville and ceremoniously sacked on the spot. In no uncertain terms, and with great theatrical aplomb, he told me that I had disgraced the world of the theatre saying, "You have upset my wife Lily, who is distraught. Now get out. You're fired. Go."

I stammered a reply, "Mr Denville, you haven't paid me for last week yet."

He barked back, "Don't change the subject, you're sacked. Just go."

I said, "Alright Mr Denville, I'll go if you want me to. But I'll need the fare home, I'm skint."

"Don't be a silly bugger," he boomed, "I haven't got your fare home."

I asked, "What shall I do then?"

After a long pause, he replied indignantly, "Well I suppose you'll bloody-well have to stay." That was the first of several occasions that Charles Denville sacked me, a scenario we would end up playing over again and again.

In Charlotte Hastings' play *Bonaventure*, Lily Denville played a young nun who, for no reason at all, wanted to sing a song in the middle of the play. Lily had a terrible voice and couldn't sing a note. Still, we got over this minor hiccup by using a record of Ave Maria instead, which she lip-synched to. It was my job as ASM to operate the record player. There were very few tape recorders in those days, and certainly we could never afford to buy one. So, I had to use an aging wind-up gramophone off-stage in the wings along with a crackling old record at 78rpm. To make matters worse, I was also appearing in a small part and had to sit for most of the action in the grate of a fireplace on the set watching this woman sing.

The operation was carried off with split-second timing; during a scene-change, I had to rush off stage through the grate and put the record on the player, set it going and then hurry back to take up my position as the gnome in the fireplace as the curtain rose again. For the first few days of the production, everything went well, and the record worked perfectly. Then, one night disaster struck. In my haste to get back on stage during the performance, the gramophone needle slipped and stuck on the record, with the singer repeating one line over and over again. Poor Lily was left high and dry, singing the same word, because it was impossible for me to leave the stage and change it. I was always in full view of the audience, and my only means of escaping into the wings meant climbing through the grate of what was meant to be a raging fire. But how could I leave Lily giving her all, miming to this awful noise? So, I felt I had no option but to slip through the fireplace off-stage, where I tried to save the day. I was too hasty and jerked the needle off the grove. It made a terrible screeching sound like a cat wailing and jumped forward to a later part of the song leaving Lily in a state of shock and dumbfounded. The audience fell about laughing. Next morning, once again, I was ceremoniously fired by Charles Denville and reinstated later when he realized he had no money for my fare home.

In one play, we were doing a barnyard scene and I decided as the ASM that it would be more realistic to have real animals, even though it wasn't required. So, I went to the local pet shop and told the owner I wanted two ducks, which he had, but he said he wanted them back at the end of the week. He really didn't want to give these ducks away, but with my cockney charm and the promise of two comps (complimentary tickets) to see the show, I persuaded him. When I got back to the theatre, I now had to play this scene where I was in the background playing a tramp – a bit like going

A SOUVENIR of the famous DENVILLE COMPANY OF PLAYERS,
at the Little Theatre, Aberystwyth, 1957.

Back Row : George Sinclair, Jeremy Hyhams, Jerry James.
Second Row :
Leonard Graham, David Davies, Maude Foster, Billi Hammerberg, John Evitts, Michell Tregarthen.
Front Row : June Lewis, "C.D.", Lily Denville, Wendy Clifford.
TO YOU WE SEND OUR LOVE,
C.D.

*Charles & Lilly Denville and the Denville Company of Players*

back to being an extra all over again – while the leading man had a long speech out front. Halfway through this dramatic monologue, the ducks started squawking, making a terrible racket, and wouldn't stop. In trying to calm them down, I only made things worse by putting my finger to my lips telling them to shush, which made no difference to the ducks but rather amused the audience. Afterwards, the leading actor complained to Charles Denville and we had the same scene over again. So, we didn't use the ducks anymore. I put the two ducks in the yard at the back of the theatre, but one tried to escape up the drainpipe and got his head caught and died. Yet still, I took both ducks back to the pet shop owner and presented them to him as I thought in my mind, although one duck was dead, giving him back two ducks was better than just one! Needless to say, the owner was really upset, and he told me never to come back to his shop again. But because of the comps he did still come to see the show, albeit with two cast members missing... the ducks!

One day the police came and asked for Charles Denville, telling him that one of his actors had been found on the beach with one of the local lasses. Denville said, "How do you know it was one of my actors, dear boy?" The bobby said, "Well, it was the cockney one, with the yellow socks." Well, there was only one person in Aberystwyth who wore yellow socks. In fact, I was probably the only person in the whole of Wales who wore yellow socks. Because in those days, what was fashionable in London, if you were a Teddy boy, took years to get up north. So, yet again, we played out the same scenario with Charles Denville telling me, "You're sacked," and me replying, "I haven't got my train fare home," and him saying, "Well you'd better stay then." The next production we did was John Patrick's play *The Hasty Heart*, the story of a soldier who befriends an insufferable Scotsman who has only days to live. Richard Todd famously played the lead role in the film in 1949. I was called upon to play the smallest part in this play as always, a fella called Blossom, who was black. In those days, there were very few actors of colour around, apart from the strikingly handsome Harry Belafonte of whom I was a great fan, and Dorothy Dandridge who was a wonderful actress. There were certainly none in Aberystwyth. So, I had to find the right kind of makeup. It was Charles Denville who came to my rescue with some valuable advice on how to prepare the makeup. "It's easy son, to play the part of Blossom you wear black socks, black mittens and mix a portion of black cork and cocoa then slap it all over your face. It works a treat," he said. It is strange to think you could get away with that in those days, today there would be an uproar, and rightly so. Charles Denville actually made up this mixture for me himself, and I duly followed his instructions and slapped it all over my face. The action for *The Hasty Heart* takes place in a wartime hospital ward, where a Scottish soldier discovers he only has a short time to live. Powerful stuff. The leading man started his big speech in the barrack room, and I was behind him, as Blossom, with my face in my hand lounging on the bed. I'm looking out to the front, of course, listening to what he's saying as it's a big, long speech. But as it was so long, I felt myself starting to nod off. Then after a few minutes of being under the stage lights, my face started to harden like embalming fluid. The mixture was squeezing my face so tightly, it was painful. Then midway through the lead actor's speech, which was so dramatic he had the audience in the palm of his hand, I suddenly felt half of my face fall off. There it was in a pile on the floor. And there I was with half a black face and half a white face! So, it was me who invented The Phantom of the Opera mask a long time before Michael Crawford! Once again, the audience were uncontrollable, and I got the sack. Thankfully, Charles Denville didn't have my bus fare home, so I stayed on and completed the summer season, which was a wonderful experience for me.

When the season finally ended, I went back home, and Billie came with me, and we found a flat in Brixton which wasn't far from where I lived in Dulwich with my parents. We continued to see one another. I never heard of any of the other actors again professionally, including the leading man who thought he was God's gift. Other than me, the only one who found any fame was my girlfriend Billie Hammerberg, who at the end of our relationship went back to Australia and became famous in *Prisoner Cell Block H*.

# 6: Actors Workshop

On returning back to London after my time in rep, I got the job of understudying Brook Williams in Dodie Smith's play *These People, Those Books*. Being the understudy meant that I rehearsed the play and knew it back to front, so that I could take over in the eventuality that Brook Williams might be taken ill during the run of the play. But he never was. I learned from an early age that the acting fraternity never, ever let the understudy on. It just wasn't done, just in case the understudy might be better. Nowadays, it is completely different. You are unlikely to get a star in the West End playing any matinee or Monday night.

I was also the ASM, which felt rather like being back in rep. I was sweeping the stage, taking the cast tea in the interval etc. It was the ASM's job to make sure nothing was left in the dressing rooms at the end of the run. I had so many half-used bars of soap, it was a long time until I ever had to buy one again.

Sarah Churchill, who was Winston Churchill's daughter, was also in the play. I recall she had to do a quick costume change, so she went behind a partition backstage. I used to go up into the gantry, so I could look down as she changed. It was quite a task to get up there and, because it was so high up, I couldn't get any more than a glimpse of her boobs from a distance, but for a hot-blooded young man, it was a highlight of the show for me at the time!

My most memorable encounter happened early one morning while I was sweeping the stage ready for the evening performance, thinking about Billie who I'd left back in Brixton. I heard a voice from the stalls say to me, "I wish I was the person you were thinking of". It was Binkie Beaumont, the famous manager and theatre producer. I had no idea who he was at the time, but he was the cofounder and managing director of H.M. Tennent Ltd and one of the most powerful people in the West End. I must have made an impression because years later, it was Binkie Beaumont who cast me as Jesus in the hit musical *Godspell*.

The gay fraternity found me attractive, and I made the most out of it and enjoyed the adulation. I can't remember exactly how I met Peter Reynolds, he was a star in his own right, famous for playing gangsters in the likes of *Guilt Is My Shadow*, although he was as camp as Chloe! I used to go to parties at his house in Swiss Cottage. He had this big room set up with a bar. I'd never seen a house with a bar in it before. Next to his party room was another room, and beyond that was a room where his mother lived. She was never seen. She never came out of that room; she was just mysteriously there. Peter Reynolds threw lots of quite risqué parties, always lots of girls there and you could use the bedroom if you wanted to. That's where I first met Dennis Hamilton, Dors' first husband, he was behind the curtain in the bedroom, 'blimping' as we called it; waiting for any action that might take place in the bed!

After a while, Peter Reynolds suggested he manage me. I was new to the business, I'd just come out of rep having learnt my trade, and to have a film star like that representing me was a big thrill. As a film fan, he probably seemed like a bigger star to me than he would seem to ordinary people. I remember he once took me to meet Roger Moore when Roger was in *Ivanhoe*, and he often took me to film sets when he was making films. This is when I realised the industry wasn't all glamour. I was once sitting in his dressing room when, to my surprise, he got in the wardrobe and said, "If the third assistant comes in asking for me don't tell him I'm here." Soon after, I heard the third assistant calling, "Mr Reynolds, we need to get this shot in before we wrap today." I then realised what he was up to. If you're on a daily rate, which he obviously was, and the shoot runs into the next day, then you get another day's work out of it. It was a bit of a shock to me that a star of this magnitude would go to such great lengths to get another day's work. That took the gloss off him a bit, but it was a great learning curve being with him.

Peter Reynolds was a close friend of Patrick Holt, who was another big star at the time, and he ended up taking over my management eventually. Holt & Dors had met while making *A Girl, a Boy and a Bike* in 1949, which also featured Anthony Newley with whom Dors had a passionate affair. Holt was married to Sandra Dorn, who was a sort of Diana Dors clone. I once overheard Patrick Holt on the phone to a casting director asking if there was anything for him in this particular movie. After they'd said no, he then asked if there was anything for the lovely Sandra Dorn, only to receive no to that as well. He persisted, asking if the film might be using any animals because he had a well-trained dog. He was told no again. Finally, almost as an after-thought, he said he was looking after a young actor by the name of Jess Conrad and asked if there might be anything for him. The casting director must have recognised my name and asked if I was the boy from the *Daily Sketch* advert, to which Holt said indeed I was. So, in 1958 I was cast in my first speaking role in *Further up the Creek* starring Frankie Howerd and directed by Val Guest. I had worked with Frankie Howerd as a film extra and his stand-in, and now here I was in an acting part in a film with him, although we were never called on the same day. This was my first film appearance after having said goodbye to being a film extra in *Serious Charge* and my time in rep.

What I didn't know then, but I do know now, is that Peter Reynolds and Patrick Holt were part of 'The Collection', the inner circle of Diana Dors' famous friends. I hadn't yet met Dors, who was still in America making *The Unholy Wife* with Rod Steiger, with whom she had an affair. As Hollywood is like a village, that affair didn't go down well to say the least, particularly as Steiger, who was Jewish, was already married. So, it didn't do Dors any favours in the eyes of the showbiz fraternity. Furthermore, in August 1956, Dors held a star-studded party and invited Hollywood columnists Hedda Hopper and Louella Parsons to interview her at the Hollywood home of her friend, the celebrity hairdresser Teasie Weasie Raymond, the Nicky Clarke of that era but even more flamboyant. The guest list included Doris Day, Eddie Fisher, Zsa Zsa Gabor, Lana Turner, Ginger Rogers, John Wayne and Liberace, who much later became a good friend of mine. Legend has it that not long into the party, one of the photographers, Stuart Sawyer, eager for a good picture, lined some of the partygoers up next to the pool. Louis Shurr, Dors' Hollywood agent, her dress designer Howard Shoup, and Dors and her then husband Dennis Hamilton ended up being pushed into the pool. After which, Hamilton emerged soaking wet and hit the nearest photographer he could find, before being restrained. The headlines in the *National Enquirer* the next day read: "Miss Dors Go Home – And Take Mr. Dors With You." This ended Dors' career in Hollywood. I always understood from Dors, years later, that Hamilton was the instigator of a prank that went terribly wrong.

I found myself back in Legrain coffee shop, the actor's hangout, and I was now able to apply for my Equity Card and find acting work. During my time in rep, a new wave of actors emerged; the likes of Jack Palance, Rod Steiger, James Dean and Marlon Brando, who brought a sense of reality to acting with which I could identify, being a boy from Brixton. One did not have to speak with such a plummy voice or dress in such a formal way. Gone were the days of suits and ties. This was the era of gritty realism.

Times were a-changing, in my search for knowledge I found out about a place which taught the method, based on Stanislavski's teachings; a set of techniques used by actors to portray emotions on stage by putting themselves in the place of the character. So, I enrolled in The Actors Workshop, the equivalent of Lee Strasberg in America. I was welcomed with open arms when I told them about my previous experience as a film extra and in rep. The workshop gave me a wonderful insight into acting because it taught me the way to break down a part and find the truth in what the play means. I would have an objective in every scene, and I was so excited that I could continue with my quest to learn my trade. I was thrilled to study with like-minded people; the likes of Steven Berkoff, Shirley Anne Field and Harry H. Corbett etc.

It was around that time that I found out that there was a stumbling block in me joining Equity because, strangely enough, there was another actor called Gerald James. When I explained this to my drama coach, he had fun asking the class to come up with a name that I could use. I must explain, you could not in any way become a star in those days with a name like Arnold Schwarzenegger. It would be unheard of. You had to have a name like Tony Curtis, Rock Hudson, Tab Hunter; a name that looked good on a marquee. At one time, I almost called myself Jed Knight as Knight was my mother's maiden name. But my drama coach didn't like it. They all called me Jess at school because of Jesse James, and my drama coach said I conjured up a vision of the adventure writer Joseph Conrad. So, when we came up with Jess Conrad my classmates all cheered and carried me around the classroom on their shoulders, because they thought it was such a great name. So, Jess Conrad was born.

So, I now had my name, my next quest was to find an agent. Well, in fact, I was lucky enough that the agent found me. Monte Mackey came to see me in a play in a theatre in Hammersmith. She was scouting for talent. She was a well-known agent from the Al Parker Agency, which was one of the biggest agencies at the time. They had James Mason, Moira Shearer and Richard Todd, who was probably the biggest star in England then. Al Parker's office was in Mount Street in Mayfair, a prestigious address. It was the most luxurious agency I'd ever been in. To get to her office, you got into a plush lift where you were transported slowly, and what seemed magnificently, to her office. There, Monte Mackey sat at a beautiful desk surrounded by flowers. She seemed to have a big crush on me, which I thought was no surprise.

So, I started doing parts in plays in theatres and on TV, the likes of *Four Just Men*. Things seemed to be falling into place. I always thought my success

*Me, with Monte Mackey*

was because of my good looks and I would say things to people like, "Monte Mackey saw me and fancied me," when actually she probably saw me and thought I had talent. Something I never thought I had. Basically, I am an introverted extrovert.

I did commercials for Bristol Cigarettes and The Daily Sketch, which was the most-read newspaper in England at the time. My friend Kenneth Hume, who later married Shirley Bassey, happened to be the director. Kenneth, who was gay, had taken me all over the continent in the past as his companion. I had become a great asset to him because he could take me to the outrageous gay clubs where within minutes of our arrival, we would be surrounded by an array of pretty boys attracted by my good looks and presence. Then Kenneth could take his pick of the available talent, leaving me to do my own thing, which usually meant finishing up in bed with a beautiful woman. It was a great ploy and worked well, and so he repaid me by giving me a fair amount of work. As the news vendor in The Daily Sketch commercial, I had to stand outside Marble Arch, where coincidentally I'd been selling flowers out of a box years earlier, and I sang the song, "Extra, extra, read all about

*The* Daily Sketch *advert that made me famous*

it in the Daily Sketch," with a ding and a smile. I made a great impact, and teenagers wrote in to ask who I was.

At the time, the TV Producer Daphne Shadwell was looking for an unknown actor to play the part of a pop star Barney Day in the Play of the Week, *Rock-a-Bye Barney*. She was looking for the perfect face and had been searching for several weeks to no avail, until she saw me on television extolling the certain virtues of a daily newspaper, at which point her search came to a sudden end, and I was offered the part. I was plucked from obscurity and chosen to play the lead role in Play of the Week, which was a big deal then as there were only two channels, so it was watched by millions. Everybody watched it. She needed to cast somebody who would play the best-looking pop star in the world. The story of *Rock-a-Bye Barney* involved a photographer, played by the Canadian actor Paul Carpenter (who seemed to be the only actor in England with an American accent, so he worked continually), who was asked to put together a composite picture of the perfect face. Instead of going for the easy option, he just took a picture of his handsome younger brother who, in his opinion, fit the bill. That younger brother was me.

At the end of the play, I was supposed to sing a song at the London Palladium. In rehearsals, everything had gone very well indeed, and I was confident. So, I asked the producer if I could use my own voice instead of miming to a prerecorded tape. My request was turned down as I was told in no uncertain terms that I was an actor, not a pop star. They used Garry Mills' voice (who went on to have a hit with *Look for a Star*), although little did they know that life would imitate art as I was soon to become a pop star myself.

*Rock-a-bye Barney* proved an enormous success and I suddenly found myself a star overnight. The very next day after it aired, every newspaper in England had the headline, "Who is Barney Day?" I was the new rock 'n' roll sensation. I received a whole stack of fan mail from teenage girls from all over the country. I was also becoming very much in demand for concerts. Moss Empires even wanted me to undertake a British Theatre Tour in the character of Barney Day, but I turned it down. I had never contemplated a singing career. I had appeared on television in a play and commercials, and gained valuable experience on stage in repertory. I was a legitimate actor now, singing was the last thing on my mind.

Shortly afterwards, I went to see Jack Good, who was the Simon Cowell of his era. He produced TV shows like *Six Five Special, Oh Boy* and *Boy Meets Girls* which at the time were the biggest pop programmes on TV.

I had an idea. I wanted to suggest to him that he might be interested in me being the compère on one of his hit shows. I didn't know quite how to handle all the fan mail I was receiving from teenagers. It wasn't that much of a surprise, because all my life I had been popular with women. But I thought there might be an outlet for me in rock 'n' roll, and wanted to get involved. Jack Good seemed the answer. He was a very shrewd operator. He was a Svengali-type character, a motivator and one of greatest image makers in the business. It was he who put Gene Vincent into black leather. It was him who gave Johnny Kidd an eyepatch to hide his nasty squint. It was him who took away Cliff Richard's sideburns and made him stop imitating Elvis Presley. He brought American stars to the UK like Gene Vincent and Eddie Cochrane, mixed them up with the English stars, like Adam Faith and Cliff Richard. At the time, he was rehearsing in a church hall in Chiswick Green and I walked in, caught his eye and said to him, "I'm Jess Conrad."

He said, "Everybody knows who *you* are!" because I was all over the papers.

I said, not really knowing what to say, "I thought perhaps I could compère one of your shows?"

Then he said to everybody, "OK fellas, let's wrap it for today, see you at 10:30 tomorrow." They all walked out of the door, Eddie Cochrane one side, Gene Vincent the other, and I remember thinking he's dismissed all these great rock stars to talk to me!

He eyed me up and down and asked simply, "Can you sing?"

To which I replied, smiling with an embarrassed chuckle, "No, I can't sing no, but I am a great mover." Au pair girls used to take me to Paris and we would win jiving competitions.

He said, "I'd like to audition you and put on a record." I used a broomstick as a makeshift mic and sang an old Bobby Rydell number. After I'd finished, Jack looked pensive. "You were right," he said, "You can't sing. But you have a certain teenage appeal. I'll make you a star by next weekend."

"But, what about my voice?" I asked.

"It doesn't matter, Jess. I don't want your voice," which I thought was a strange thing to tell someone who was on the verge of a pop singing career, he said, "I want your face." Jack, however, was so sure he called me *The Face of the Sixties*.

The next day, my agent rang up and said in her plummy voice, "You know, darling, that you auditioned for the Young Vic, well they want you. Your contract will say 'play as cast', which means, darling, that you'll carry a spear in one production and in another production you will have a few words. Very, very good for your acting career. Or… a man called Jack Good has phoned and wants you to become…" And she stumbled as the word 'pop' wasn't known then. She was struggling to get the word out. I could hear her young secretary in the background prompting her. She continued, "…oh yes. He wants you to become a pop star. So, what is to be, darling? Would you like to go to the Young Vic, which would be so good for your acting career, or would you like to become one of these pippety, poppety, pop stars?" She couldn't even spit it out the second time. So, I said, "I'll become a pop star, please," and that is what I did.

# 7: Golden Boy of the 60s

Rehearsals started almost immediately. We went up on the train from London to ABC Studios in Didsbury where they filmed the likes of *Boy Meets Girls* and *Wham!* every week with the compères like Keith Fordyce, and American rock 'n' roll star Eddie Cochrane (hit song – *C'mon Everybody*) etc.

When it came to music, we looked to America for the lead and copied everything the Americans created on the rock 'n' roll scene. Billy Fury and Marty Wilde were Britain's answer to Elvis Presley, and Jack Good was looking for an English counterpart to Fabian, a great looking pop star of the time who was more famous for his looks than his voice. When he saw me, Jack Good knew he had got his man. I was the English Fabian.

That weekend, I made my debut on *Oh Boy!* where I sang a duet with Billy Fury called *Chick-a-chick-a-honey*. Billy Fury's name didn't mean much to me then because I was more interested in becoming an actor; I really had no aspirations in this thing called pop, knowing nothing about it other than it was happening. I certainly didn't mind being part of it, however! I didn't realize quite how famous Billy Fury was, he really was the English Elvis. Jack Good, genius brain that he had, put me right next to Billy to see how the girls would react to this new boy on the block. All the adulation didn't throw me, like it probably would another newcomer, because I was used to being adored by women all my life. I was the best-looking boy in the school, a dashing Teddy Boy with a lot of swagger, then I became this heartthrob housewife's favourite repertory actor, so being a pop idol was almost the natural next step.

*Billy Fury, Jess Conrad, Gene Vincent, Joe Brown, Eddie Cochran, Adam Faith and Marty Wilde*

Billy & I shared a dressing room. It was a very odd friendship, me being a cockney boy and him being a lad from Liverpool, but I guess what we had in common was that we were both posers, which is what you become when you're born with good looks. On one occasion, he was getting ready for a show and I asked him how he gave his hair the Elvis-look. He showed me how he soaped his hands up and ran the soap through the sides of his head leaving the top untouched. So, I was starting to learn all the tricks of the trade of being a popstar, and Billy and I became very good friends.

I admired him greatly and used to watch him performing from the wings. He was not only a good singer, but he also had stage presence and knew exactly how to put over a song to wring out just the right kind of emotion from the lyrics. I once saw him actually crying on television when he sang one particular tear-jerking song, and I thought what a great actor he was. I was impressed. It wasn't until later I found out that he had a raw onion in his top pocket which helped to bring on the tears!

After the show, we went back to our hotel and I heard a noise. There were girls in the wardrobe. I said to Billy, "You didn't tell me about the chicks, man!"

He replied, "Yeah man, lots of chicks," as we called girls in those days. They were everywhere, under the bed, in the wardrobe…

After that one appearance on television, Jack Good was true to his word and put me on *Wham!* and *Boys Meets Girls*, which were so popular that at six o'clock every Saturday night, the streets were empty as the teenagers were all glued to the box watching their idols. Jack Good was an unsung hero in many ways. Although he was famous at the time, he was very unique and so creative. We were all rough diamonds, he was dealing with Cockney boys, people from Manchester and Liverpool, and yet he was a real toff, very public school, but he had this incredible insight into what the teenagers wanted. He knew how a rock 'n' roll star should be. We were so rehearsed. It was unbelievable, but it was hard work. We had three cameras and on a certain line, you would have to turn to one camera and wink, and then you'd turn to another camera and snarl. And if you missed an angle, wink or a smile, Jack Good wouldn't talk to you for a week. The whole thing was choreographed down to the last detail. It was like acting, you had to project your image. Gene Vincent was the devil, dressed in black with a green light on him. Whereas, when I asked Jack Good what my image was, he told me; my image was a young boy walking through a cornfield, drinking a glass of milk, a typical boy-next-door. I said, "Thanks Jack," and thought to myself, *what can I do with that?*

I signed a recording contract with Decca Records and over the next few years I enjoyed several Top 20 singles including *Cherry Pie*, *Mystery Girl*, *This Pullover*, *Every Breath I Take* and *Pretty Jenny*. Within six months, in 1961, I was voted Britain's Most Popular Male Singer by the New Musical Express, beating the likes of Cliff Richard, Marty Wilde, and Billy Fury. The NME was the number one music paper of the time, the publication everybody took notice of. I was so popular, I needed two secretaries to look after my fan club.

I toured the world with many of the legendary stars of rock 'n' roll; Gene Vincent, Eddie Cochrane, Billy Fury, Marty Wilde, and Jerry Lee Lewis, and we had an absolute ball on tour. There were so many hilarious incidents, so many funny stories, and so many girls flocking after us. I once made love to two girls in a cupboard in the middle of a press reception, with the reporters and photographers just a few meters away outside the door. I sacked a drummer because he was playing too softly. "Why are you sacking me?" he complained bitterly. "You're not playing loud enough. The audience can hear *me!*"

I once played a terrible trick on heartthrob Heinz, whose hits included *Just Like Eddie*. Halfway through his act, during an instrumental break in the middle of one of his songs, he used to sprint off stage, run out through the stage door and into the car park and then rush around to the front of the theatre. Through the front door, he would then hurtle down the auditorium

*A blank membership card in case you have lost yours*

47

through the audience, and leap back on to the stage while the band continued to play the instrumental. On this occasion, however, Heinz was singing the song and building the number up to fever pitch. It was going really well; the audience was loving every minute. When it came to the group's instrumental, Heinz set off on his marathon, charging off stage into the wings and out of the theatre, where I caught him and held him there for at least fifteen minutes before I let him go back on stage again. The band repeated the middle eight at least seventeen times before he returned.

Following on from the most popular rock 'n' roll shows of the day, *Wham!*, *Boy Meets Girls*, and *Oh Boy*, and being voted England's Most Popular Singer by the NME, I guest starred in *Dixon of Dock Green*, which was a bit of a cultural turnaround and somewhat of an achievement. I jumped straight back into drama by being cast in what was then one of the most-popular, gritty dramas on TV. I played a biker, which was right up my street as I wore my own black leather and a colourful flowing scarf. It was just by chance, by studying the method and having seen Brando in Wild One, that everything seemed to be falling into place.

The filming location was the Ace Café, which back then seemed to be in the middle of the country – it is actually on the North Circular Road near Stonebridge Park in London. I remember walking in there and hearing my latest record playing on the jukebox, which at the time seemed surreal. After we had shot those scenes, it was back to the studio in West London for interiors, where I was to meet one of Britain's most popular film stars, Jack Warner. As an extra I used to watch the actors. Now as an actor myself starring alongside Jack Warner, I was always interested to observe how fellow actors worked. In those days, if a show wasn't live, it would be taped as live continuously, which meant that you'd film in sequence from start to finish and any mistakes would have to be left in. During one of my scenes, one of the walls of the set collapsed. We continued as if nothing had happened.

Later on during the filming, disaster would strike again. The trademark of *Dixon of Dock Green* was for Jack Warner to deliver a long monologue at the end of each show, summing up, rather like a moral sermon, something that the viewing audience looked forward to. I was watching when halfway through his speech, he dried. He literally froze and forgot his lines. There is always somebody there standing in the wings with the script ready to prompt you if this happens. It was obvious he was struggling to remember the words, but he would not take the prompt. You could see the strain on his face. So, he was prompted for a second time, but he still didn't take the prompt, and his face showed more and more distress. It upset me to see this well-respected actor agonisingly go through this, which would have been so visible to the television audience at home.

Although my episode of *Dixon of Dock Green* has not been seen since 1961 and is presumed wiped, the legacy of my episode still lives on. As the first celebrity to be associated with The Ace Cafe, in 2019, I was called upon to attend the 60th anniversary of the 59 Club, the British Motorcycle Club, at St Paul's Cathedral. The place was filled with long-haired bikers dressed head to toe in leather, along with tourists and passers-by, and my heart was in my mouth as I stood before a packed house and read an excerpt from the New Testament.

The first film where I had billing was *The Ugly Duckling*, a Hammer Film Production in 1959. It was directed by Lance Comfort and starred Bernard Bresslaw, who by this time was one of my closest friends, having played charity football with him for years with the TV All-Stars along with the likes of Mike & Bernie Winters and Alfie Bass. Others in the film included Jon Pertwee, Richard Wattis, and David Lodge, with music supplied by Joe Loss and his orchestra. The film was shot at the *Locarno Dance Hall* in Streatham which later became *The Cat's Whiskers*, *The Ritzy*, then *Caesars Nightclub*. I didn't have far to go, a hop and skip away, as at the time I was living in Dulwich Village. It was probably the closest and most convenient film location I ever had.

Bernard Bresslaw was one of the hottest actors in the country, owing to his starring role in ITV's *The Army Game*. I played the leader of a gang of Teddy Boys; I called my character Bimbo after my brother Richard James,

*Dixon of Dock Green Disc Magazine, January 1961*

who later became an actor himself. I had a fight scene with Bernard Bresslaw, which I played as realistically as I could, as always. All things considered, it was a good cameo part for me, and at the end of the film every character had a walk-down on-screen during their credit. Like many of my films, *The Ugly Duckling* is enjoying a new lease of life today on Talking Pictures TV.

Also around that time, my next film was *Friends and Neighbours*, made by British Lion Films in 1959, a comedy written by Talbot Rothwell who went on to write the *Carry On* films, set in the height of the cold war about a working-class British family who entertain two visitors from Russia. It starred Arthur Askey, who was one of the last music hall stars and one of our best-loved names. With the likes of Tommy Steele, Frankie Vaughan, and Cliff Richard, all of whom starred in films around that time, the influx of the new generation began to filter into British movies and the producer thought it would be a great idea to have the so-called old guard meet the new guard. I was quite aware, at the time, that I was cast for my box office appeal as teenagers made up a big percentage of filmgoers.

I played Buddy Fisher and was required to sing, obviously, as that always seemed to be part of the plot then. The film also starred a young June Whitfield, who befriended me. It was the first time a member of the opposite sex had shown an interest without, as far as I know, any sexual motives. June and I continued to be close friends right up until she sadly passed away aged ninety-three, in 2018.

One of the standout memories of the film was when I was required to play a scene with a portly well-known character actor called Ken Parry. Upon being introduced to me, he was all a fluster. When we rehearsed, things got worse. He couldn't look at me, he dried. He seemed completely overwhelmed by my presence. This carried on take after take. He couldn't get a line out; he was dripping with sweat and his face became more and more ruddy. He was in a right two and eight. I personally felt very sorry for him, and was relieved when the director suggested that I leave the set for his close-up so that I was no longer in his eyeline. I was used to fans acting like that, but I was surprised to find that a trained actor would act the same.

Strangely enough, I never did get to meet Arthur Askey, the star of the film, as so often happens if you don't share a scene together. For years to come, on hearing I'd done a film with him, people would often say, "Wow, what was Arthur Askey like?" and I would make up stories saying he was brilliant, although I never met him. "Great fella." "He was terrific." "Great laugh." But I'm sure he was all of those things.

In 1960 I starred in *Too Young to Love*. It was made by the Rank Film Organization and shot at Elstree, where they now film *EastEnders*. The film was based on the play *Pickup Girl* by Elsa Shelley and directed by Muriel Box, who was very keen to use me at the time as I was probably the most popular person in the industry, having such a large teenage following on the back of my success as a pop star. Before the film started, Muriel Box used me to audition at least six of our up-and-coming British film actresses to play opposite me, including Susannah York.

When filming commenced, I was surprised to discover that the actress that they had picked to play opposite me wasn't in fact any of the talented and beautiful young British actresses that auditioned, but an unknown actress from America called Pauline Hahn.

Thomas Mitchell was also in the film, who I was, of course, terribly excited to meet. He was one of the finest character actors of the time, who I had seen in numerous Hollywood movies including playing Vivien Leigh's father in *Gone with the Wind*, the film that made her a star, and playing the doctor in *Stagecoach*, which made John Wayne a star.

Having been a member of the Actors Workshop, I was very interested to observe the way Thomas Mitchell worked. He was always the first person on the set. I noticed the way he handled his props and was a consummate professional, a complete opposite to Victor Mature. Playing opposite him throughout the film was a great experience for me, and I learned a lot from him.

In this movie, I was required to play the violin and the film company put me in touch with Albert William Jeffery, who was the partner of Rita Webb, a well-known character actress who, incidentally, I already knew. I would go to their house and he taught me how to play the violin, something that took a great deal of time and practice to achieve.

Unfortunately, the film, in my opinion, was ahead of its time and generally shocked the audience and did not do tremendously well at the box office, but didn't seem to harm my popularity. It has now found a new lease of life on Talking Pictures TV, as have many of my other movies. Pauline Hahn was a sweet young actress who I went on to date.

# 8: Meeting Miss Camay

Just after I had made my first hit record, *Cherry Pie*, Phyllis Roden, who was a well-known casting director at Pearl & Dean, was throwing a party which I was invited to. As she was a casting director, I invited Billie Hammerberg, who I had been seeing since my days in rep, and now lived with in Brixton. I also invited the leading lady from my latest movie, Pauline Hahn, as I was seeing her off and on, on the guise that we were doing publicity. Plus, I was also working the room, something that became second nature to me over the years. Many years later, Jim Davidson would often make a thing of saying to people at parties, "Watch Jess work the room." It always started with a smile, which seemed to make people go weak at the knees. Nature gifted me with a whiter set of teeth than everybody else's which, along with my confidence in my own looks and personality, would ensure I would pretty much take over any social gathering.

I couldn't help noticing a beautiful girl who, if you had to put a label on her, was an Audrey Hepburn-type as opposed to Marilyn Monroe. Most of the women up until that time I had dated were beautiful, showbizzy, vivacious, outgoing types. This creature seemed to be self-contained and oozing class. The first thing I did was smile at her, which usually dazzles them. I put my arm above her head, onto the wall, and leaned in and said, "It's a bit crowded now, but I'll squeeze you in. Do you fancy coming out some time?" and she said, "Maybe. When you get rid of her, her, and her," pointing to each of the girls at the party I had been chatting up. So, she had obviously been observing me. Her tactic was to get me to pay serious attention to her, and the way she did that was to pretend to be indifferent. She seemed to have called my bluff and, I thought at the time, this wasn't going quite as well as I expected! So, I retreated with my tail between my legs back to what felt like safe territory, working the room.

The day after, I was booked onto a commercial for Vespa scooters directed by my friend Kenneth Hume. The call sheet had me report to a small studio in Brighton and I was the first to arrive, as I usually am, and I was having a

*Top model Renée Bergmann*

*"You look a little lovelier each day with beautiful pink Camay"*

mirror check when in the reflection I saw a face I recognised peep round the door saying, "Fancy seeing you here!" It was the girl that had given me the cold shoulder the night before. Kenneth Hume then formally introduced us and told me she was the model Renée Bergman and she would be playing my girlfriend in the commercial. Renée was the daughter of a Dutch air force officer, who was killed in action early in the war in Indonesia. With her mother and sisters, she went to a prisoner of war camp, eventually reaching England when she was seven. She had just left stage school and was trying to make it as an actress. She was eighteen, I was twenty-two. The first shot was set up and Renée was sitting behind me on the scooter. I said, "I'm sorry all you can see is my back," and she said, "Never mind, your back is better than most men's fronts!" and that was the start of our romance.

When Kenneth set up the shot, he said, "I want you to drive the Vespa down the ramp to the beach," at which point I told him that I couldn't ride a scooter. As I was famous and we were mates he said, "Well, you'll just have to do the best you can," as if to say we are in this together. So, I reached for the throttle and catapulted off, crashing onto the beach. Somehow, with some jiggery-pokery and Kenneth's ingenuity, we completed the commercial.

At the end of the shoot, I suggested I take Renée home in my car, which was a red MGB sports car with wired wheels; a top poser's car, which I hoped would impress her. We drove with the roof off, stopping at the newly built Gatwick Airport, which was the place to be at the time. In those days you could just leave the car outside, walk up the steps into the lounge and have milk and a dash. I remember people there were remarking loudly on my yellow socks. Little did we know, it was the day of the official opening by the Queen, which made it even more of a memorable occasion.

With her middle-class background, Renée gave me my first taste of class. She introduced me to plain chocolate and dinners for two. Until now, I had always gone home for tea with my mum. Renée was the first really sophisticated girl I'd met. Eventually, she became Miss Camay *"You look a little lovelier each day with beautiful pink Camay"* advertising the soap on television for three years, until her face became almost as well-known as mine.

# 9: Konga

Now that I was a film star, I no longer had to audition for films. Films were offered to me. In 1961, I starred in *Konga*, made at Merton Park Studios, which was my neck of the woods because as a teenager I spent many evenings pulling birds at the Wimbledon Palais. Filmed in technicolour and produced by Herman Cohen, who was well-known for making horror movies, *Konga* was the British version of King Kong. Instead of taking Fay Wray up the Empire State Building, Konga took me, the obligatory pop star, up Big Ben! I was to be working alongside Michael Gough, who was one of the most famous names in the horror genre. My love interest was played by

*Konga is a notable example of Herman Cohen's SpectaMation cinematic filming system*

**Don't Miss....**

# 'KONGA'

in Eastman Colour and SpectaMation

starring

| Michael | • | Margo |
|---------|---|-------|
| **GOUGH** | | **JOHNS** |
| Jess | • | Claire |
| **CONRAD** | | **GORDON** |

Executive Producer   HERMAN COHEN

Screenplay by ABEN KANDEL & HERMAN COHEN

Directed by JOHN LEMONT

**ANGLO AMALGAMATED
FILM DISTRIBUTORS LTD.**

JESS CONRAD

stars in "KONGA" an exciting spectacle filmed in Eastman colour and dramatic SpectaMation for release by Anglo Amalgamated Film Distributors Ltd.

*The lobby card for* Konga

Claire Gordon. who at the time was having an affair with Tommy Yeardye, one of Diana Dors' exes, although the publicity mill would have the public believe that she was having an affair with me. All good publicity for the film. The film also featured one of the first screen appearances of Steven Berkoff, with whom I had studied at the Actors Workshop, playing a member of my gang.

On the first day of filming, I remember actress Margo Johns being introduced to a young Konga, played by an actual chimp who immediately got a hard-on which apparently was bought on by the aroma of her perfume. The apologetic handler said how sorry he was that this had happened, to which she replied, "No, I'm rather thrilled. A man hasn't been this excited by me for many years!" Things got even more surreal when, to make sure it didn't happen again, the handler chased Konga all over the set, only to finally catch up with him and give him a hand job!

It was decided, as I had an enormous fan following, that I would sing in the movie and the song would be my latest release, which was called *This Pullover*. At the time, it was quite normal for pop stars to sing about things like *Blue Suede Shoes, Kicking Up the Leaves, Pillows to Cry On* etc. So, singing about a pullover, which incidentally were very popular at the time, didn't seem odd at all. In fact, on the release of the record, teenagers sent me hundreds, perhaps even thousands of pullovers, mostly hand-knitted, in all different colours, which I then had to distribute to various *Oxfam* shops in person as I had so many. Given that I was going to sing this song in the film, the wardrobe mistress came up with a horrendous looking, fluffy, over-the-top pullover which I wouldn't normally be seen dead in, which I was required to wear all the way through the film.

I remember I had a tremendous fight scene with Michael Gough which was quite a bundle, made even more believable because of my realistic acting technique. But, the trooper he was, he never complained.

One day, my now fiancée Renée came on the set at teatime to visit. As I was the star of the film, I was quite surprised to find that the producer Herman Cohen was uncommonly offhand, for reasons only known to him. Perhaps he didn't want to think of me as being straight, given that he was a gay man.

When the film was finally released, I was surprised to find that the song *This Pullover* had been cut without my knowledge. By the time I found out, it was too late to do anything about it. Such a shame as Kenny Everett, on his very popular radio show, would go on to vote *This Pullover* as the world's worst record, and therefore, the world worst record could have been in the world worst horror film, which would have been great publicity and given the film another cult dimension. So, as they say in the business, they missed a trick there and in fact made me go through the film in a ridiculous looking pullover for no reason whatsoever.

*Konga* is so bad it's good, and over the years it has built a tremendous cult following and has been shown all over the world, and at film festivals, and on television. Talking Pictures TV shows it regularly. On numerous occasions I have been invited to watch it at events in person, I always get a standing ovation and the film gets an amazing reception. It has to be seen to be believed!

When I went to America to promote *Konga*, I stayed at the Gene Autry Hotel on Sunset Boulevard in West Hollywood. When I got to my room there was a note together with an apple and a banana on a plinth which said, "Welcome to the Gene Autry Hotel". I immediately phoned my mum, which in those days could take some time. I finally got through her and said, "Mum, guess what?"

She said, "What?!"

I replied, "Gene Autry's only left me an apple and a banana, that's all." She cried over, "Dad!". He shouted, "What?!"

She said, "Gene Autry's only gone and left Gerry Boy an apple and a banana," to which he remarked, "Another bleedin' poof!"

While I was in Hollywood, Herman Cohen told me he was going to take me up the canyon to meet Tab Hunter. Tab was a matinee idol, like Tony Curtis, and had great success in films like *Battle Cry*, *Damn Yankees*, and *Gunman's Walk* and had an enormous fan base of teenage girls. Naturally, I was obviously very excited about meeting such a big screen idol, although I wasn't quite sure what to expect. What I didn't expect was what happened next.

When the door opened, Tab was standing there in a plastic apron which had suspender belt and stockings and a pair of huge tits on it! It wasn't exactly the image I had imagined from one of the most macho Hollywood leading men. He invited me in to join the party and meet the gang. Inside I was confronted by William Bendix, certainly not a matinee idol; he was more famous for his gangster roles. He was dressed in stockings and high-heeled shoes, and he said to me, "Hi Jess," and I remember his wrists effeminately gesturing, "My word, you are an attractive boy!" Tab then announced that Tom Tryon, another screen heartthrob, was in the kitchen making apple pie, "especially for me." So, there I was surrounded by what I thought would be masculine screen idols, but in fact it was the opposite. As we sat down for a drink, Tab was insistent, "All you Limeys are gay!" and then like a roll call he reeled off names, "Dirk Bogarde, John Gielgud, Alan Bates..." who I must admit wasn't on the obvious cast list. I told them I was mentally gay but not physically. Tab said, "Oh, I thought you were, as I saw you checking every mirror as you came in!".

Then, having had a drink or two, somebody rolled a joint and that was passed around. It didn't take much time for me to realise that, in their minds, I was going to be the dessert! Being aware of the situation I was in, I suggested that as I hadn't seen anything of Hollywood, that maybe we could go out somewhere and return later. So, that is exactly what we did. They took me to a club which they called the 'Hole in the Wall Club'. When I arrived, I was surprised to find that through these holes, bums appeared. One could slap these bums, kiss them or one could do whatever one liked with them! I did think for a moment, I would have been better off staying at Tab Hunter's and taking my chances! At one point, a backside appeared, and Tab exclaimed, "Ahh, Rock's here again!" I naively said, "Rock who?" and he replied, "Rock Hudson". I asked him how he knew it was Rock Hudson and he said, "Oh, he's always here. I recognise the blemish on the left cheek!"

After a while, having seen enough bums popping out of holes in walls, I decided to do a Houdini and said that I was going for a mirror check. I got to the exit as fast as my legs would carry me, called a cab, and got back to the Gene Autry Hotel. When I got to my room, I took a deep breath and thought to myself, if this is the first night in Hollywood, I dread to think what is going to happen next.

# 10: Rag Doll

In 1961, I made a film called *Rag Doll*, produced by Blakeley's Films, which went to America as *Young Willing and Eager*. The director was Lance Comfort, who had also directed *The Ugly Duckling*, in which I was featured. Now in *Rag Doll*, I was the star and I still hadn't said more than two words to Lance Comfort, with whom I was making my second movie. I always thought the important thing was to turn up, know your lines, and do the job as opposed to making the director your best friend, which I now realise actors did.

We shot at Walton-on-Thames studios, which I was so thrilled about because that was where I used to live and parade around as a Teddy Boy. And now here I was, starring in a movie. It would seem that the parts I was playing represented exactly who I was in my West End days. Someone who was on the wrong side of the law, and at odds with society, so therefore I drew as much as I could from past experience, as Stanislavski would have us do.

*Rag Doll* tells the story of a young girl who escapes the bad life in a small town, only to find something far worse in the big city. My love interest was Christina Gregg, who had been a famous model, rather like Miss Camay. *Rag Doll* also starred a very fine actor called Kenneth Griffith, and Hermione Baddeley who was a famous theatrical figure and showbiz personality at the time. She never stopped making passes at me. I remember on a take, she actually groped me under the table. Being the pro that I was, I valiantly continued with the scene, which shocked her, because it was supposed to have put me off, and brought a smile to the director's face.

In the film, I sang *Why am I Living?* which was to be my single when the film was released. They always had me sing a song that they planned to release as a single, although they had made the mistake of cutting *This Pullover* out of *Konga*. The backing band were the Dave Clark Five, who were film extras at the time, but later became as famous as the Beatles.

I was so thrilled to have a dramatic death scene, that I made sure that it lasted as long as possible, à la James Cagney in *White Heat*. I can only

*A daring story of today's youth…*

imagine that men, not my biggest fans, watching in the cinema, would be shouting at the screen, "Hurry up and die you ****!"

The film, all in all, was a great experience and is still being shown today on Talking Pictures TV.

# 11: The Queen's Guards

*The Queen's Guards* was a really big deal, it was made by 20th Century Fox, whose iconic fanfare I would later use as the introduction music for my concerts. I was the first to use it, but is now used by all and sundry. *The Queen's Guards* tells the story of some soldiers who undergo rigorous training and discipline to qualify for the honour and prestige of becoming royal guards. The Queen herself gave her permission for the crew to film the Trooping of the Colour, which included my character.

The Queen's Guards *Billboard*

*Above and right: publicity stills from* The Queen's Guards

Shot in Cinemascope and directed by one of the world's top film directors, Michael Powell, famed for his partnership with Emeric Pressburger. Powell had directed films including *Black Narcissus* and *The Red Shoes*. He was a celebrated, iconic film director, to some on the same level as Alfred Hitchcock. Michael Powell could be very brusque with actors but I had a kind of cockney thing that Tommy Steele and Michael Caine and Joe Brown have. Boys from South London have a kind of brashness, if you like, we're outgoing and we can give as well as we take. If he said something to me, I'd say something back to him. He was such a famous director, I even knew that at the time, but I had no fear of him and he realised that, and I didn't try it on so much.

The film starred Raymond and Daniel Massey, of the famous acting dynasty. I received Special Guest Star billing. Naturally, the poster proudly announced: Jess Conrad sings. The song I sang was *Oh Caroline,* which I wrote. They always assumed that pop stars could write songs. I couldn't, but gave it my best shot.

The film's publicity had me putting up an enormous poster in the Haymarket where the film premiered. It was a proper West End film premiere, so much so that I took my mother as opposed to my girlfriend who by now was used to pretending to be different girls to the press, but had run out of wigs!

A Scene from the 20th Century-Fox release
"THE QUEEN'S GUARDS"
In CinemaScope · Color by De Luxe

Printed in the U.S.A.

This film was on a different level to anything I had done film-wise before. The film had lots of action and was very physical, which I really enjoyed. I was instructed to go to Kensington Barracks, where I was fitted for my guard's uniform which included a Busby which, you wouldn't know unless you have ever had to wear one, weighs a tonne. Together with the uniform, this was one of the most uncomfortable costumes I have ever had to wear as an actor. I was taught to march up and down by a recruiting officer, who looked upon me as a recruit rather than a film actor and gave me a terrible time, although in the end I never actually had to march in the movie. There were, of course, long shots of me marching, but they were done by a 6ft 1 double.

Instead of using the Gobi Desert, the film was shot in Camber Sands which has a big stretch of sand in the coastal resort of Hastings. I remember us all getting together the night before in the local hotel, where I met a very amusing man, who I pointed out had two odd socks on, which caused some amusement at the time. I had no idea at the time that he had a wooden leg and had forgotten to change the sock before he came down to dinner. He told me that he was going to be in a scene the next day, which puzzled me as I didn't recognise him as an actor and wondered what sort of contribution he was going to make. The next day on location, I saw him in combat uniform arrive at the trench only to be blown up revealing that the blast had taken his leg off, when in fact it was in the prop cupboard!

On another occasion, after long and arduous set up for an enormous battle scene, there were lots of army fellas there and just before the take the director shouted through his megaphone at the top of his voice, "Would somebody please tell our celebrated pop star to stop smiling, we're making a war movie!"

*My mum and me at the premiere*

# 12: K.I.L. 1

I went from *The Queen's Guards*, a cinemascope spectacular starring showbiz royalty, the father and son duo Daniel & Raymond Massey, to *K.I.L. 1*, a black and white melodrama with part of another famous acting dynasty, son of acting icon Leslie Howard, Ronald Howard. As I had carte blanche on casting, I of course cast the man who got me into showbusiness in the first place, Larry Taylor, and his son Rocky who by this time was my stand in and double, and was also involved as second assistant director. At the time, Rocky did look very much like a young Jess.

Made by Eagle Films, the producer Stanley Long said that Christine Keeler was in the film, but he didn't call her on the days that I was involved as he was frightened that I might get off with her, which at the time I thought was outrageous. As one of the most sought-after men in the industry, I certainly wouldn't have given her a second look.

The film was shot in a small studio in Brighton and the surrounding area, which made it a pleasant three-week shoot. The plot involved a scrap dealer who was making a profit out of wrecked cars, but then trouble starts when one of his men demands more money.

There was one hilarious moment when Rocky who, as my double, had a fight scene with his father Larry. In the rehearsal, they worked out exactly how the fight was to be choreographed and then on the magic word 'action', Larry hit Rocky through the glass window knocking him unconscious. I thought to myself, this is why us stars need doubles! The punch would have put me in hospital for a week.

The film went to America and became *The Skin Game* but has since disappeared into obscurity. I have never seen it, but would love to.

# 13: The Boys

At last, I was cast in something that looked as if it was going to be worthwhile. In fact, it has turned out to be a cinema classic. Sometimes, in this business, it is who you know, not what you know, and at the time I was friends with Mike & Bernie Winters. They invited me to a party at which was Sidney J. Furie, who unbeknownst to me was a film director, and had seen me there relaxed and being 'just Jess'.

The next day, my agent at Al Parker, Monte Mackey, got the phone call saying that Sidney J. Furie would like to cast me in his latest film, to be called *The Boys*, which was to star film star Richard Todd in his last film under his studio contract with ABPC, and marked his last major movie.

*On-set of the British Film* The Boys

*The Boys* was shot at Elstree in black and white for its gritty realism. The thing at the time was to shoot in colour for musicals and black and white for drama. We filmed exteriors at The Peabody Buildings in Paddington a week before they were demolished. It was the first film I made where realism was the most important thing. This was Britain in transition; pre-Beatles, pre-sexual-revolution 1960s, where boys still wore smart suits and went to dance halls for a good time. *The Boys* mixed courtroom drama with kitchen sink realism, and the story involved four Teddy Boys who are put on trial for the murder of a garage night watchman. The film begins with their appearance in court and their plea of "not guilty", and then through flashbacks pieces of the story come together, leaving the viewer to make up their own mind as to whether the boys are innocent in spite of what seems conclusive evidence.

The early 1960s was a time of great moral panic regarding the rise of Teddy Boys and juvenile delinquency in Britain, and the film plays this out. Richard Todd played the prosecuting counsel, and Robert Morley played the defence counsel. Robert Morley turned out to be a remarkable companion; he treated us like his own sons and would take us out for tea and cakes along Borehamwood High Street. Rita Webb, whose partner Albert William Jeffrey had taught me how to play the violin in *Too Young to Love*, played my mother. There are guest appearances by the likes of Wilfrid Brambell, Roy Kinnear and Carol White, with music provided by *The Shadows*.

On the first day of filming, the boys played by Dudley Sutton, Ronald Lacey, Tony Garnett and I met and it turned out I was the oldest one. As I'd been a Teddy Boy, as opposed to an actor having been to RADA, I based my character Barney Lee on a younger version of myself. As the fashion was changing from drape suits to the Italian look, I took that on board and went for a light suit knowing that it would stand out. I also used a cigarette holder, which as a Teddy Boy I did so that people took more notice of me, and I wanted this character to be hopefully the only one they looked at and dressed accordingly.

*A publicity shot of four well-dressed lads*

70

One of our first scenes was an ensemble including Robert Morley and *The Boys*. On observing the rehearsal, the director Sidney J. Furie said, "You know what you're doing. Rip up the script and improvise," which suited us and Robert Morley, but was something that Richard Todd found very difficult to grasp. Sidney J. Furie came back half an hour later and we shot the first scene, and that was how it was to be for the rest of the shoot.

Although the film was going for realism, it still had a sense of humour. At the time I was known as the Pepsi Cola kid, as I had a very successful advert on television selling Pepsi Cola. In one of the café scenes in Soho, there's a subtle nod to that as the set designer actually hung a poster of me advertising Pepsi on the wall, which brought a smile to my face.

On one occasion I noticed Sid Furie looking at himself in a mirror, and instead of making himself look neat and tidy he took some time dishevelling himself. The tie had to get loosened, the hair got ruffled, he clearly wanted to look like a rag bag, not a smart young film director. So, I think he too was taking a step towards being real, as opposed to the likes of Hitchcock, who was always smart in a three-piece suit with collar and tie. So, the whole thing was realism even down to the director.

*The Pepsi Cola kid*

After making this film, Sidney J. Furie flew to America to direct Marlon Brandon in *The Appaloosa*. Brando was obviously adept at the method and would have been on the same page as Furie. There is no doubt that Sid Furie was a great director and brought out great performances not only from *The Boys*, but the other cast members. I used a lot of my past life experiences in the film as I had been a Teddy Boy in the West End in real life and thoroughly enjoyed every moment of being in the film. *The Boys* was widely praised by critics for its realism and standout performances and has become a classic. It is still a must-see today on Talking Pictures TV.

On 17th September 2017, the 55th anniversary of the film's release, the three surviving Boys including myself, Tony Garnett and Dudley Sutton, met for a reunion screening of the film at Elstree Studios where the courtroom scenes were filmed, which was organised by Renown Pictures who distribute the film. It was the first time we had all met since the making of the film. I still looked the youngest and it was a wonderful reunion. Within a short space of time, we lost Dudley Sutton and Tony Garnett. It is sad to think now that I am the only one still alive.

*Reunited with the great Dudley Sutton*

*Elstree Studios' Morris Bright with* The Boys *Tony Garnett, Dudley Sutton and me.*

# 14: Armchair Theatre

In 1963, I was overwhelmed to be cast in *Armchair Theatre* opposite the biggest female star in the world, Carroll Baker. At the time, she had eclipsed Marilyn Monroe in her 1956 smash hit film, *Baby Doll* and was now going to come to England to star in an episode of play of the week called *Paradise Suite*. I was always interested in what would lure Carroll Baker from America to England, and it was only later that I realised that it may have been because this episode was based on the life of Marilyn Monroe.

*Paradise Suite* also featured the up-and-coming Ian Holm and Sam Wanamaker, who I instantly clicked with. I remember he had a Zippo Lighter which I thought was the ultimate macho-man's accessory, and the in-thing to have at the time. So the cast was filled with all top-drawer actors and directed by Philip Saville, one of the most sought-after drama directors at the time. I remember him giving me very little direction, from which I took from that I was obviously doing a good job.

*Armchair Theatre* was shot in the ABC studios in Teddington, and on meeting Miss Baker it was obvious that she was method through and through, as was Sam Wanamaker. So, we were all on the same page and it was a very harmonious group. The story revolved around a famous Hollywood star, yearning for love, who seduces the bellboy at the hotel she is staying at, played by me. My costume was a tight-fitting, streamlined bellboy's outfit which showed off my best assets.

Given that they couldn't show us having sex on screen in those days, the metaphor for our intimacy was us over-gyrating dancing the twist in a hot jiving session, at the end of which Carroll Baker appears to have enjoyed an orgasm. Every time we rehearsed the scene, her husband Jack Garfein, a producer himself, would comment, "This is a masterpiece!" and the viewers and critics seemed to agree. The programme made the front cover of The TV Times and rated over eighteen million viewers, making the Top 5 programmes of the week. Clifford Davis of The Daily Mirror said in his review: "Pop Singer Jess Conrad makes an impressive debut."

*A publicity still from Armchair Theatre*

*Another publicity still from Armchair Theatre*

# 15: The Human Jungle

On the tail of playing opposite one of America's greats in *The Paradise Suite*, in 1963 I was asked to play opposite one of Britain's Greats, Herbert Lom, in *The Human Jungle*. Herbert Lom was another actor who I realised was working from the same system that I was, the method, so I was completely relaxed.

My episode *The Flip Side Man* revolved around Danny Pace, played by me, who was a successful pop singer and recording artist whose career was beginning to suffer. He is convinced that he can see his doppelganger, and that somebody is out to sabotage him. It took a lot of homework on my part before I started filming because I had to explore quite deeply schizophrenia, which I did by reading up on it and talking to my doctor. Some things I had to do as the character were off-the-wall, and the fact I had done my research meant that by acting in certain ways I wasn't fazed by it, as I knew it would be how my character would react.

I also had some difficult stunt work to do so, of course, I made sure that Rocky Taylor, who not only looked like me but was a well-established stunt man, doubled for me once again. Although I said I would prefer to do some of the stunts myself, even though in doing so I could have ended up hospitalised. One of the stunts that the director insisted Rocky do for me was a very dangerous stair fall. On the day of filming, I suggested to Rocky that he should wear pads on his arms and legs, which at the time he seemed to pooh-pooh. I said to him, "You're not Superman, even if you think you are." So, wardrobe supplied him with padded gear, and after he did the scene he received a round of applause from the camera crew and agreed that without the pads; he would have ended up doing great harm to himself.

*The Human Jungle* was filmed in Beaconsfield studios, and I stayed in a pub for the duration. Although Brixton wasn't a long drive, I wanted to keep myself in the zone so to speak. It was hard work, but acting alongside Herbert Lom was a great experience, as was being directed by Sidney Hayers who went on to direct *The New Avengers* before heading to Hollywood.

*In* The Human Jungle

Once again, I would sing in this production. After which, I released an EP containing the songs *It's About Time, I Don't Care (What People Say), One of These Days* and *Down Town Tonight*. I used my own band led by Rhet Stoller, who was my musical director and a very talented musician.

I remember as a teenager I was always fascinated by watching villains die on the screen. As I seemed to die in all my films, due to playing the bad boy, and because the death scene seemed like such an important moment, I remember eking it out by contorting my body into realistic shapes, so it was memorable pictorially and the camera stayed on me as long as possible. As death scenes go, it was one of my better ones.

*The cover of the 45*

It was a case of art imitating life, because the agent in this episode was a woman, who looked like my agent then Monte Mackey, and acted like her in as much as everything I did, my agent had to approve of. In many ways, once again, there were lots of similarities in my life. If you are well cast, you will find lots of things that are similar.

Many years later, when I was at a celebrity lunch, Herbert Lom, who obviously knew I was going to be there, took the time to come over and speak to me. He bought over pictures of our time together on *The Flip Side Man* to show me. So, I must have made an impression all those years ago. I look upon him as a true icon of British cinema.

# 16: Aliki, My Love

My agent phoned to say that producer George St. George had shown some interest in me making a film in Greece. The star was to be somebody called Aliki, who I was told was Greece's equivalent to Marilyn Monroe. In other words, a Greek megastar.

The next thing I was told was that Aliki, whose full name was Aliki Vougiouklaki, wanted to meet me in person. So, I was flown to Athens at the film studio's expense. On my arrival at the Kings Palace Hotel, I was told, "Aliki has requested for you to go to her room." When I arrived there, it was obvious by her attire that my audition as such was going to be of a physical nature. I realised then, that if I didn't please Madam Aliki I wouldn't get the part, and thought it's a long way to have travelled for the old casting couch ploy, but I had to see it through. I must have been satisfactory, as I was cast as the male lead, Barry Wilson.

*Aliki, My Love*

*The Island of Happiness*

I played a rich American playboy who inherits an estate on a remote Greek island. When I visit the island to deal with my inheritance, I meet a charming local girl played by Aliki, along with her devious mother, and my life changes completely.

At the time, Aliki monopolised the press with stories about her affair with Prince Constantine II, who later went on to become the king of Greece. Now that I had arrived, all the papers asked, "Who will she choose? The Prince or the Pop Star Jess Conrad?" and this went on for a considerable time, with film stills of us canoodling posted alongside pictures of her and the prince. It only trailed off slightly when we went on location.

The film was shot on the island of Ios. All my films up until that time had been so diverse, and this was my first stab at light comedy à la Jack Lemmon. I was, of course, required to sing and Manos Hadjidakis, who was the most-famous Greek composer, was to provide the musical score. I didn't realise then how different Greek popular music was compared to British and American. It was like chalk and cheese, as I was soon to find out.

*With Wilfrid Hyde White*

The director was Rudolph Maté, one of the pioneers of film noir in the 1940s, and had directed the likes of Tony Curtis, Barbara Stanwyck, and Edward G Robinson. Sadly, he was now at the end of his long and illustrious career, but obviously still knew his way around the block.

The film would also feature Wilfrid Hyde-White, who was an iconic English comedy actor having starred in films such as *My Fair Lady*. He was a great joy to work with, although many a time we were sent home for corpsing as we were unable to finish a scene where something inconsequential made us laugh. The next day, we would start where we left off and have the same difficulty all over again. So many happy memories of us behaving like naughty boys, but it couldn't be helped.

It was agreed before filming that my wife would come out and visit me at the film studio's expense. She did, and as she was a top model and had become famous as Miss Camay getting out of the bath, she was immediately offered the part of my secretary when we were filming interiors in Athens. However, upon release of the film, Aliki made sure that her part was cut out.

Ios was a fabulous island, then untouched by tourism. I had mentioned in passing that I loved the beach on which I was living in a small property. They said that I could buy the beach for fifty pounds. But, as it involved bringing in a lawyer from Athens, I thought *what do I need a beach for? I'll never come back here.* Can you imagine a beach in Ios for fifty quid? Certainly one of the greatest mistakes I have ever made in my life, and I've made a few.

I often wondered why, given the beautiful location, the film was shot in black and white. At the time, I spoke to Cliff on the phone, who was making *Summer Holiday* in glorious Technicolour in Athens, and I told him about my movie and had to admit to him that mine was being shot in black and white, and neither of us could understand why. On further investigation, I was told that Finos Films only make black and white movies. How ridiculous is that?

On its release, *Aliki My Love* broke all box office records in Greece, though perhaps less fortunately, because she was unknown in Britain, Aliki came and did a long and arduous promotional tour with me around all the Esseldo circuit. We must have done every Esseldo cinema in England.

*Aliki My Love* was truly the most beautiful location I had ever experienced, until my next film came along, which was to be a Cinerama film shot in Budapest…

# 17: Marrying Miss Camay

To Renée, I was like Sir Galahad. I was brought up on films and swept her off her feet. I was her knight in shining armour, yellow socks and all. On one occasion, we had decided to drive my adorable MG through France to Spain, which meant flying from Lydd to Le Touquet, a route that no longer exists. Renée's mother disapproved of our relationship and did not want her daughter to marry a Cockney pop star. Her family had her marked out for a perfect English toff, a stockbroker-type, a *Hurray Henry*. So, on finding out that we planned to drive to Spain, she got in touch with Interpol and told them that her daughter was running off with an undesirable, which made me laugh because I was the biggest pop star in Britain at the time. Renée got a phone call at Lydd airport saying in no uncertain terms that if she didn't come home immediately, she shouldn't come home at all. Renée was so frightened she was trembling. But we continued our journey, and when we got back Renée was forgiven, like all prodigal daughters. I left all the arrangements to Renée and was told that we had rented a villa in Palamós. After a fabulous two-day journey, we finally arrived there. Now, this was in the early days of international tourism, when renting was a new thing, and the villa was flea-ridden. We somehow found a way to laugh about it. At least we seemed to have shaken off the police!

We had a fabulous time; empty beaches, fabulous food for very little money, and I achieved one of my ambitions at the time; to see a bullfight, which was acceptable in those days. It is traditional for the bullfighter to cut off the ear of the bull and throw it at the most attractive woman in the crowd. He threw it to Renée, who later bought it back home only to find that years later the dog found it and ate it!

As a popstar in the 60s, I did all the things my agent told me to do. "Don't drink in public," said my agent who had to maintain my 'boy next door' image. So, I was never seen with anything stronger than a glass of milk in my hand. "Speak properly," said my agent. So, I took elocution lessons to cultivate the hillocks and troughs of my South London accent. "And

*On our wedding day*

whatever you do, don't get married," said my agent, mindful of the romantic delusions of record-buying young girls. I had told my agent that I wouldn't. Though unfortunately, some things are easier said than done. and during my time as a pop star Renée and I were secretly married in Holland, in a town where Renée's grandparents lived. If the news had ever got out, it could have ruined my career. Renée bought a number of coloured wigs to enable us to go out together in public. She would often accompany me to film premieres and parties, wearing a different wig each time and sporting a different name so that nobody ever realised it was the same person. It was easier to get away with what we were doing as the paparazzi wasn't anything like it is today, in fact the phrase paparazzi was unknown. The press photographers and public thought I was going out with a string of different girls, and we managed to keep our marriage a closely guarded secret.

Before we got married, Renée had found us a house in the evening newspaper. A half-timbered, cottagey place near the old Pinewood Film Studios in the showbusiness suburb of Denham in Buckinghamshire, which acquired the name of Little Hollywood. At one time Cilla Black lived next door. Patrick Mower was across the road. Roger Moore, until he moved to Monaco, lived nearby, and then Paul Daniels and Debbie McGee moved in.

We managed to keep our wedding secret for two years, a feat helped by my frequent absences from the pop scene while pursuing my other career as a film actor. Renée stayed at home, dealing with the fans who found their way to the front door, and pretending, if pretence was called for, to be my secretary / housekeeper. It wasn't until Renée was seven months pregnant with our first daughter Sasha that an official announcement became necessary. When the Beatles came along and John Lennon was married, then with the stroke of a pen it became OK.

# 18: Panto Debut – Jack & the Beanstalk

I love Pantomime. It conjured magic for me. I adored the great pantomime performers of the past like Nat Jackley, Arthur Askey, and Arthur Lucan who was Old Mother Riley. Christmas is one of my favourite times of the year, because it allows me the luxury of appearing in pantomime, and I starred in many seasonal productions during my career in the provinces and in London. One thing of which I am certain is that I can bring a lot to pantomime, because it has been ingrained into me from my early days as a kid, watching pantos during the war. I grew up with it, and nowadays I come to the medium with great knowledge about the art and not as some uninformed pop star.

The Dame being played by a man is set in stone and would never change, and quite rightly so, but there became a time when Prince Charming being

Jack & The Beanstalk *at Westcliff-on-Sea*

played by a buxom woman and kissing a pretty Cinderella seemed to become old fashioned to the public. I was one of the first male actors to play Prince Charming, and it would seem I had all the boxes ticked. I was a pop star, therefore top of the bill material. I was tall, dark, and handsome and was famous for having a good physique and good legs. You must have good legs to wear tights, and I have particularly good legs owing to my natural physique, and the fact that I played football every Sunday and worked out.

My first major engagement in pantomime was in 1963 at the Palace Theatre in Westcliff-on-Sea, where I starred as Jack in Jack & The Beanstalk. Roberta Pett played the comedy lead, Simple Simon, a part which should by that time have been played by a male comedian. As times were evolving, it didn't look right that they'd been modern in casting me as Jack, a part that was usually played by a woman, yet they'd cast Roberta Pett, the producer Jerry Jerome's wife, in a part that should have been played by a man. I remember Alan Wells being quite magnificent as the Dame. The pantomime was such a success that it had an extended run, which I have to say was happily the case with most of the subsequent pantos I did, and I must have starred in about fifty over half a century.

# 19: The Golden Head

In 1964, I found myself in yet another incredibly interesting location, Budapest. The iron curtain had just been lifted and the government was anxious to encourage tourism, so we were treated like royalty.

During the six-week shoot, I was shocked to see that nobody had cars on the road except for high-ranking politicians. On a couple of occasions, I visited people's homes and the only pictures on the wall were not works of art, but photos of cars and we were told whatever we did not to tell anybody that we had cars. There was always a government official in the room, the whole situation was macabre.

The film was originally going to be called *Milly Goes to Budapest* and was to star Hayley Mills and Lionel Jeffries, but due to film bosses being unhappy with the original director James Hill, filming ground to a halt, those scenes were scrapped and a new director, Richard Thorpe, was brought on board. Thorpe was an enormously famous veteran Hollywood film director who had directed the likes of Burt Lancaster, Joan Crawford, Debbie Reynolds, Fred Astaire, and even Tarzan Johnny Weissmuller. Like Rudolph Mate who directed my previous film, Thorpe was also nearing the end of his career.

The film's plot involved British youngsters in Budapest attempting to catch the thieves of the golden bust of Saint Laszlo. I played the juvenile lead, Michael Stevenson.

During the filming, all anybody wanted to know about was what it was like filming in Cinerama. All I did was say my lines and hit my marks. As an actor I wasn't interested in what cameras they used, although everybody seemed to be more excited than me. It was as if I was going to be the first man on the moon! Cinerama was a widescreen process that originally involved projecting three synchronised 35mm projectors onto a huge, deeply curved screen, thus giving the audience a surround effect. Therefore, the film could only be shown in cinemas with the right equipment. The only place in London was the Royalty Cinerama Theatre in Holborn. One was overwhelmed by the film being shown in the round, as it were, but as the

screen was so huge it was very difficult to camouflage the joins in the three screens, with visible cracks down the middle.

The film was to star the famous veteran Hollywood actor George Sanders, who was always complaining about his fee as it was going towards paying alimony for his ex-wives, and Buddy Hackett who was a well-known typical American zany film comic. The film also starred Robert Coote with whom I became very close friends, so much so that Renée and I asked him to be godfather to our daughter Sasha.

My love interest was played by Cecília Esztergályos, a beautiful young Hungarian actress, who seemed to be waiting for me to make the first move, which I never did. It is always better to not get romantically involved with your leading ladies. It saves a lot of kerfuffle.

Renée made her usual visit, as it was always in my contract that my wife should come on location at the film company's expense. She brought along extra nylon stockings, which were much sought after in Hungary, and impossible to get there. Renée had a fabulous time sightseeing, what with the Danube being slightly more pictorial than the Thames!

Once again, I was asked to sing and of course the song would be released as a single. But this time, having learned a lesson from *The Queen's Guards*, I bought in a very famous song writer who was also one of my best friends, Mitch Murray, who had a great track record in writing hit records for the likes of Freddie & the Dreamers, Georgie Fame, and Manfred Mann. Mitch came over and we had a great time. *Things I'd like to Say*, the song he wrote for the film, was not a hit but was released by Columbia Records. I had more records released in my films than Henry VIII had wives!

The film had a big black-tie premiere on 8th April 1965 at Royalty Cinerama Theatre in Holborn. I remember an unknown comic coming along who just happened to be being looked after by my publicity agent, Eric Braun, the then unknown Roy Hudd.

After that, I didn't see the film for forty-five years until in 2007 when I was flown to the Schauburg Cinerama Kino in Karlsruhe, Germany to attend a screening at the 70mm Film Festival. Over the years, I have made numerous other appearances when the film has been screened at festivals. In 2016, I made a personal appearance at Widescreen Weekend at the Pictureville in Bradford in 2016. Like many of my films, by this time I was one of the last cast members standing. The hot topic of conversation, once again, was the Cinerama camera!

# 20: 1964 Panto

In 1964, music producers having seen the success that pop stars had starring in pantomimes, decided to jump on the bandwagon. Unfortunately, they didn't have the background and experience of the artform that is pantomime. Everybody thinks things are easy until they try them. I was cast alongside pop singer Millie in *Once Upon a Fairy-tale*, which was billed as 'a new pop style pantomime spectacular'. It wasn't a famous pantomime story, but more of a hybrid of pop-meets-panto. We were to play cinemas rather than theatres, starting at the Adelphi Slough and moving on to the Granada

*In* Once Upon a Fairytale

Bedford, Maidstone, and Mansfield. I had high hopes for the production, but it was a complete disaster. The producers failed to even mention Jimmy Wheeler (catchphrase "Aye aye, that's yer lot") on the publicity poster, and he was one of the biggest variety stars. I wouldn't be surprised if he held the record of playing the Palladium more than any other comic. Millie, who had found fame with the hit song *My Boy Lollipop* was not an actress, and you have to be to perform well in pantomime. Having no theatrical training, when she delivered her lines, she tended to speak too quickly and the audience couldn't understand a word she was saying. It was very difficult to give her notes, and to add to that the director Harry Dawson had no panto experience. So the whole thing was a disappointment and was buried after one season.

GEORGE COOPER ORGANISATION LTD. PRESENTS:—
A NEW STYLE 'POP' PANTOMIME *SPECTACULAR!!*

# ONCE UPON A FAIRYTALE

STORY BY JIMMY WILSON · DEVISED BY HARRY DAWSON · WORDS AND MUSIC BY HARRY DAWSON AND JIMMY WILSON.

COMMENCING DECEMBER 24th AT THE
**ADELPHI, SLOUGH**
ALSO GOING TO GRANADA BEDFORD, MAIDSTONE AND MANSFIELD.
*(Watch Local Musical Papers for Details)*

DECEMBER 26th TO JANUARY 2nd AT
**GAUMONT DONCASTER**
4th-9th JANUARY
**ODEON NORWICH**
11th-16th JANUARY
**ODEON BARKING**
18th-23rd JANUARY
**GAUMONT WORCESTER.**

STARRING:

# MILLIE
# JESS CONRAD
# THE TORNADOS

STARRING:

# LULU AND THE LUVVERS
# HEINZ AND THE WILD BOYS

DES LANE
MACK & KIRK
ALEX MUNRO
AND ALL STAR CAST

# MARTY WILDE

ALEC PLEON
CAL McCORD
JOYCE BAKER
AND ALL STAR CAST

## TWO SEPARATE PRODUCTIONS

*A Grand Christmas Show for Young & Old!!*

# 21: The Amorous Adventures of Moll Flanders

*The Amorous Adventures of Moll Flanders* was made by Paramount Pictures in 1965 and directed by Terence Young, who directed me in my last film as a film extra *Serious Charge*. He insisted on me playing one of the Mohocks, which was an eighteenth Century version of a Teddy Boy, as I was in *Serious Charge*. I got Special Guest Star billing, and you can't say fairer than that.

The film was shot at Pinewood, so close to where I live, I could almost walk there. I had endless fittings for my costume and Rococo wig, which was really quite something and took a lot of grooming. I was asked by the casting director whether I could fence to a high standard, as if I had been a RADA student I would have. Because one says yes to everything, I said I could. The second question was whether I could ride a horse to a competent standard, which would entail galloping. Once again, I answered I could. As soon as I was cast, I immediately started to have riding lessons and I remember quite clearly that you only have to look a horse in the eye, which you usually do before mounting it, and it knows whether you can ride or not. So, as happened to me, you trot around the field and the horse always makes sure your outside leg crashes against any object it passes; fence, gate, feeding trough etc. My lessons took some time to make perfect. My backside was red raw. Bathing every night became difficult, with my wife rubbing Deep Heat into my wounds. Painful. In tandem with that, I was going to town every day to have fencing lessons. When I got to filming, the only scene shot including the Mohocks of which I was one, required us to walk with a horse holding it by its bridle. The only sword fighting was equivalent to what I would have done as a twelve-year-old on a bomb site which was 1, 2, 3, lunge. 1, 2, 3, lunge. You're dead. Absolute waste of time and money.

The film was based on Daniel Defoe's 1722 novel of the famed English adventuress Moll Flanders, and was to star Kim Novak who had famously been one of Hitchcock's blonde beauties. Also starring were Richard Johnson and George Sanders, who was still paying alimony to his ex-wives. The second Mohock was played by Noel Harrison, Rex Harrison's son, with whom I got on very well. He later had some success with the song *Windmills of your Mind* which was a Top 10 hit in 1968. The other Mohock was played by an actor called Alexis Kanner who was, as sometimes happens in my acting career, somebody that has a bee in their bonnet about me being famous. He tried to upstage me in every scene, but with my vast theatrical experience, which he obviously knew nothing about, I was up to all his tricks and he had little success. I am glad to report that he has not been heard of since!

My dressing room was next to Kim Novak's, and she had visitations every lunchtime from actor Richard Johnson with whom she was having clandestine relations. They bonked loudly, which meant there was never any chance of me taking a nap. Then she had the gall to give me come-to-bed eyes when we did our scenes together. I thought to myself, little do you know, I have already heard the Kama Sutra at full volume every lunchtime! I have seen pictures of Kim Novak recently, and it is so heart-breaking how beautiful film stars can ruin their looks with appalling plastic surgery.

The overall experience was blink and you'll miss me, but I thought to have Special Guest Star billing and do so little was typical of the film industry if they really wanted someone.

# 22: 1965 Panto

In Christmas 1965, I starred in *Puss in Boots* at the Grand Theatre in Swansea, and what a great theatre it was to have my first taste of a major pantomime. The Welsh love their pantos and this one was a great box office success. The Dame was played by Bryan Burden, who later became famous for playing the Dame at the Theatre Royal Windsor for twenty-five years. Grande and Mars were a famous double act who also starred, and an eighteen-year-old Keith Harris who later became famous for his ventriloquist act with Orville was doing his first panto, playing Puss. Little did I know that he would go onto become a household name and star in and produce his own pantomimes. I took Keith under my wing and taught him the ropes. Keith had seen how popular I was with the chorus girls, and we were in the wings watching them

rehearse some exotic dance moves one day, when he confided in me that he had never kissed a girl, or indeed ever had any sexual experience. So, I said something like, "Leave it to Uncle Jess!". At the end of the rehearsals, I took him into the girls' dressing room, which they all shared, and announced that we had been watching them rehearse and that Keith would appreciate it if one of them would show him the ropes as he had never dated a girl before. Years later, he would boast that Jess Conrad was the first person to arrange for him to get laid! *Puss in Boots* was such an incredible success that the run was extended to the end of January. John Chilvers, who ran the theatre, was pure showbusiness and I wasn't surprised when I heard that he was awarded an MBE for his services to theatre in Wales in 1973.

# 23: 1966 Panto

The following year in 1966, I starred in the title role of *Robinson Crusoe* at the Embassy Theatre in Peterborough. The dame was played by Sandy Lane and the comic was Welsh comedian Johnny Stewart. The spesh act was very of the day. Gilbert & Partner was a real gorilla and its handler who lived in a caravan in the theatre car park and was only led in to do his bit, which I

ELKAN & BARRY SIMONS present

JESS CONRAD

AS

Robinson Crusoe

AND

ALL STAR COMPANY

For a 4 weeks Christmas Season
COMMENCING MONDAY 26th DECEMBER 1966

think was only one or two entrances and walk-down. But it was extremely dangerous, as the gorilla, who was some size, seemed to be constantly sexually aroused by the chorus girls' perfume. I recall many embarrassing and dangerous situations of the gorilla chasing the girls all over the theatre! I wasn't surprised as it brought back memories of a similar situation when I made the movie, *Konga*. *Robinson Crusoe* is a difficult story to tell, as it is set on a galleon and a desert island and has never translated well into a pantomime, which is why it is now rarely done.

# 24: Hell Is Empty

In 1967, I was now with London Management and being looked after by a famous agent called Michael Sullivan who was married to former French film star Dany Robin, whose wedding I was later a guest at. Sullivan was a chain smoker and many years later he and his wife both died when their Paris apartment caught fire through them smoking in bed. Years later, I later found out I was signing cheques for my commission on various projects to Michael Sullivan, not London management, and he obviously hadn't been forwarding them on, as I assumed he would be. So, when he died, they contacted me asking for money that was owed to them which I'd paid to him. He was one of these agents who would do anything to seal the deal. He was what we would call a ducker and diver.

Now, I don't know how I got the part of Jess Shepard in *Hell is Empty*, but I recall Michael Sullivan calling me and asking me if I'd like to do the part. One of the deciding factors was that I was told that the star would be Richard Conte, the iconic Hollywood gangster figure. Michael Eland was the producer and was married to Martine Carol, who was to be the female lead. Carol was a top box office draw in French cinema. I met up with Michael Eland at his house in Regents Park. My agent did the deal, which I was happy with at the time.

Soon after, I flew out to Czechoslovakia where I stayed in a hunting lodge just outside Prague. I remember I had to go through a garden to get to my accommodation, which was a lovely apartment off the main hotel. We started to shoot the film and I travelled daily from the lodge to the location, which was a beautiful castle with all the trimmings. Wonderful grounds and peacocks, rather like a Czechoslovakian Buckingham palace.

It was really nice to catch up with Shirley Anne Field, my friend from the Actors Workshop, then a quite sought-after actress. I wondered how Michael Eland had persuaded her to take part in the film. He was quite a ladies' man though, so who knows. The actress I played opposite was Catherine Schell, with whom I would later work again when I guest starred in *Space 1999*.

Through these weeks of filming, we got very close, and Martine Carol made no secret that she too was completely besotted with me. Once again, this all sounds very big-headed of me, but it is true! As Martine Carol was the star of the film, whatever Martine Carol wanted Martine Carol got, which meant me having to be there every day on location, regardless of whether I was required on set or not. She insisted I would travel with her in her car to and from the shoot, and she seemed to be completely fixated on me. A strange situation, but a situation that I had experienced many times before. She was completely infatuated with me.

Eventually we got to the scenes that I was to star in with Richard Conte, and I would ask, "What is my eyeline?" as he hadn't arrived yet. Before long, we got to a situation where we couldn't do much more filming-wise, as we had shot everything we could without our leading man, so the production ground to a halt.

Eventually, the day finally came when our star Richard Conte was to arrive from Hollywood. As we were not shooting at the time, we all excitedly went to the airport to give him a big film star welcome. Personally, I was thrilled to be meeting such a well-known Hollywood legend and one of the reasons I had said yes to doing the film in the first place. To everyone's amazement,

from the plane came the last man you would want to be associated with at that time, through his incredibly bad reputation of being a drunk and leaving various wives in dire straits, the then washed-up Anthony Steel. For everyone concerned it was shock, horror!

I later found out that Michael Eland had been lying to us all the time and although he had thought about Richard Conte, he hadn't actually spoken to him. Or if he had, he had got "no" for an answer. It turned out that one night Eland, while having a drink at The London Hilton, had noticed a drunk Anthony Steel propping up the bar. In desperate need of a leading man, Eland asked the then seemingly unemployable Anthony Steel if he would like to star in a film he was making and fly out to location as soon as possible. Steel could not believe what he was hearing, and in a drunken stupor, of course, hastily said yes.

Before filming recommenced, Steel was told in no uncertain terms that one drink would put him on the plane home. So true to his word, he never touched a drop during what turned out to be months of filming. Before long, Anthony Steel and I were getting on like a house on fire. Being an alcoholic, he used to watch me drink a lager and the perspiration would run down his temples. He would ask me if he could hold the glass and roll it across his forehead to give him an icy, cooling sensation. This happened every night. Being ex-army, Anthony Steel immediately took an instant dislike to German actor Carl Möhner, who I have to say was a pain in the ass. Möhner had driven from Germany and therefore had his car to hand, which would seem to be his pride and joy. He'd offer you a lift to location, but the offer would come with a list of dos and don'ts; certainly no smoking and no touching the dashboard etc. He would open the boot to reveal a stack of neatly ironed posters displaying the various films he had starred in. Möhner was married to a younger wife who, on our meeting while having dinner, couldn't take her eyes off me, which really upset him. When he asked her why she kept gazing upon me, she replied, "Because he's a famous pop star", to which Carl Möhner grunted.

This film was so full of ups and downs. One day, James Robertson Justice, who was obviously on a daily rate, mentioned to Michael Eland that he hadn't received his brown paper envelope. He was then told he would get it first thing after lunch. Now, in normal circumstances, one would be surprised at this behaviour from such a well-established character actor, but on this particular production with Michael Eland, all sorts of skulduggery was happening. So, when we assembled after lunch, James Robertson Justice said something which I have never forgotten. As the director was about to call "Action", he announced in his best actor's voice, "No pay, no play." We all stood looking at each other until Michael Eland appeared and placed a brown envelope in James Robertson Justice's palm. By that time, everyone knew how slippery Eland was, and James Robertson Justice stood and counted the cash in front of us. So, we all now knew his daily rate!

The film went on for what seemed like an eternity. Renée made two visits at different times due to my contract stipulating that my wife should visit at the company's expense. I also had in my contract that I would fly home every Saturday night to play charity football on a Sunday. Thankfully, for all concerned, that only ever happened once, as it was out of season.

Towards the end of the production, Martine Carol died suddenly of a heart attack, to everybody's disbelief. What was going to happen now? The film had not been finished and, worse, everybody involved with the film suspected that it could have been foul-play by her husband, the producer Michael Eland. I would hate to think he killed her, but he was certainly under suspicion. It just seemed odd that given her age, she was only forty-six, and the fact that she had no signs of illness (other than her infatuation with me!) that she would just suddenly drop dead. In an even stranger twist of fate, I was immediately given her room, which was the best room in the hotel. At this point, Agatha Christie came to mind!

With no leading lady, the clapper boy had to dress up in her costume with the remaining scenes shot from a distance. The last scene we filmed was in a discotheque at midnight, and we were all aware this was to be the last shot in the film. Although we were all tired and working more hours than Equity would allow, we just wanted to get it in the can. The first thing Anthony did after we wrapped was to have his first drink since the film started. It was such a joy to see his face drinking that pint of lager. Not only was he having his first drink, but he had also succeeded in not having a drink throughout the whole period of filming. That look of joy and contentment on his face is something I will never forget.

The next morning, back at the lodge, I woke up at the usual breakfast time, went into the lounge and saw what I thought was Anthony Steel's back, he was sitting on a chair, and I said, "Morning Tony." He slowly turned his face towards me, in what seemed to be slow motion, and revealed what looked like a gargoyle. He was unrecognizable. He had obviously been drinking all night. He asked me, "Which room is that bastard Carl Möhner in?" and because Anthony Steel was my friend, I told him, although I shouldn't have done. Then he immediately left the room, like a man possessed, straight up the stairs to Carl Möhner's bedroom, where he kicked down the door. Carl

Möhner, in complete and utter shock, jumped from his first-floor balcony in his underpants, into his car, never to be seen again!

On returning to England, Anthony Steel was interviewed by many newspapers about this comeback to his film career, where he mentioned that he'd been so thrilled to work with this up-and-coming new boy on the block, Jess Conrad, in glowing terms; for which I will be forever thankful. Later, he went on to live at Denville Hall, the famous actors' home where I often met up with him for coffee. Like many other aging actors that lived there, even into the 1970s and 1980s, he would go to auditions and continued to work in the industry.

# 25: More Panto – 1967 & 1968

In Christmas 1967, I was delighted to return to Barnsley as a panto star in *Mother Goose*, having started my acting career in rep at The Theatre Royal. As that theatre no longer existed and was by this time a piano shop, the pantomime was staged at The Civic Theatre. Jerry Jerome cast me for the second, having been a success in Jack & the Beanstalk in Westcliff-on-Sea. This time, instead of his wife, the female lead was 'Britain's loveliest Miss World' Ann Sidney playing Colin. Ann Sidney was a delight to work with. Having paid a lot of money for the two leads, perhaps there wasn't a lot of money left for a proper goose costume, as I remember the only appearance it made was with its head sticking through the curtain and speaking a few words. The show was a great success. My wife Renée and my young daughter Sasha enjoyed Barnsley very much as we stayed on a farm for the duration of the run.

In Christmas 1968, I co-starred in *Dick Whittington* at the Ashcroft in Croydon with Jimmy Thompson, who I had never heard of and likewise he had never heard of me. Frankie Murray played Sarah the Cook. Being a South London boy, living in Brixton and Dulwich, the press had a field day (along the lines of 'Local Boy Makes Good') which Jimmy Thompson probably was not over-awed with. I was called for a costume fitting with the producer Betty Astell, who was married to the then household name Cyril Fletcher (known for his catchphrase 'Pin back your lug holes' and odd odes), as she said that she was going to have my costumes specially tailored for me, which is usual practice. She was waiting for me with a tape-measure, and she dropped to her knees and proceeded to measure my inside leg. She seemed to put the end of the tape measure unusually high, purposely brushing past my manhood. Being young and easily aroused, I found myself with a hard-on and wondered whether we were doing *Jack & The Beanstalk*!

# JESS CONRAD

STARRING IN

# Mother Goose
# Civic Theatre, Barnsley

WISHES TO THANK

**JERRY JEROME     JOHN SIMMONS**
and CO-STAR ANN SIDNEY

FOR GIVING HIM THE OPPORTUNITY OF

# BREAKING ALL CASH RECORDS

"JESS CONRAD'S SPOT PROVED THE HIGHLIGHT OF THE SHOW."
*YORKSHIRE EVENING POST*
"EXCEPTIONALLY WELL PERFORMED BY JESS CONRAD."
*YORKSHIRE POST*

"HIS BILLY GOOSE, BRIGHTEST AND BREEZIEST YET."     *SHEFFIELD STAR*
"HE HAS THE RIGHT CAVALIERING SPIRIT AND ROMPS THROUGH THE SHOW . . . SHOW OF THE WEEK."
JAMES TOWLER, *STAGE*

MANAGER:
**KEITH DEVON,**
DELFONT-GRADE ORGANISATION LTD.
235 REGENT ST., W.1.
01-734 9961

PUBLICITY:
**ERIC BRAUN,**
48 CHEPSTOW VILLAS, W.11.
01-229 4074
01-930 6644

# 26: The Assassination Bureau

*The Assassination Bureau* was another situation where they wanted me for a particular film just because the character sings a song. They thought immediately of my popularity as a pop star and agreed to give me Special Guest Star billing, and a handsome fee.

Directed by Basil Dearden and released by Paramount Pictures in 1969, *The Assassination Bureau* was a spirited caper about the self-confident chief of an association of hitmen for hire, who finds himself the target. It was inspired by a book co-written by Jack London and had an interesting cast including Diana Rigg, Beryl Reid, and Warren Mitchell.

I thought it would be a fun film to make as Oli Reed, who was a close friend, was set to star in it. I also knew Telly Savalas, who had come over to England some time before on a shopping spree with his wife and played golf a couple of times for the Variety Club of Great Britain. I got on well with Diana Rigg, and she asked me if I was interested in buying her second

*In* The Assassination Bureau

hand mini, which unfortunately I wasn't. At that time, I wouldn't have been seen dead in a Mini as I had a mauve and white Ford Zodiac with whitewall wheels.

I played the part of Angelo, a gondolier, and when I arrived at Pinewood, my favourite studio as it is so close to where I lived in Denham, the first thing they did was perm my hair and give me a very striking costume. They wanted this gondolier to look amazingly attractive, so they dressed me in a very eye-catching outfit, although it took hours to perm my hair.

When we got to the scene, the song was as far from a pop tune as you could get. In fact, it was operatic. So, the reason I was booked as a popular actor / singer went out of the window, as they would have been better suited casting an opera singer. The song wasn't melodic, and it was only heard in passing. It had nothing to do with the story or taking the character forward, but I was beautifully dressed and looked incredibly striking.

The best thing about the whole experience was the fact that lunches with Oli were, as always, memorable because he would arm wrestle me a hundred times. Then he would tell me that he would pay for lunch if I could bring any friends along to arm wrestle them. What is sad is, on Oli's last film *Gladiator*, he did just this. According to witnesses, he drank eight pints of German lager, a dozen shots of rum, half a bottle of whiskey, and a few shots of Hennessy cognac and took on a group of sailors who were on shore leave from HMS Cumberland at a local pub. After beating five much younger Royal Navy sailors at arm-wrestling, Oli suddenly collapsed, dying while en-route to hospital in an ambulance. I was upset to hear about Oli's passing as we went back a long way, even before he was famous we got up to lots of larks.

# 27: Diana Dors

When Dors returned to the UK, Peter Reynolds tried to set me up with up her. He obviously told her that he'd met me and that he thought I'd be exactly her type. Clearly, he thought this would earn him brownie points from Dors. So, I got the call from Reynolds asking me if I'd like to have dinner with her. He arranged for us to meet at a hotel on the Bayswater Road. I'll never forget the smile on her face when she first saw me. After dinner, I escorted Dors to her room at the hotel. I assumed she would pull me in, although I didn't want that to happen, but instead she said, "Oh no, not on the first night. But I'm starring at The London Palladium on Sunday and will arrange for you to be in the Royal Box." Sunday came and I was in the garden with my family, but I knew in the back of my head that I was expected at the Palladium. I thought to myself this is the last thing I need, any complications from an affair with Diana Dors! So, I decided not to go.

I had found someone who was very glamorous and who loved to be surrounded by beautiful young men. I never realised I could have a platonic relationship with a woman until Dors. She introduced me to some of the most beautiful women in the world, and was one of the biggest influences in my life. Over the years, she often visited me at my house and met Renée and the family. I accompanied Dors on many of her engagements, which I always enjoyed. As time went on, although always special, her acting roles were not as frequent as they once were. She'd gone from being leading lady to playing character parts, which she did superbly and proved what a great actress she was.

Dors had a big house in Sunningdale to maintain. Andrew Ray, who was a famous actor, lived there. She had live-in boyfriends who came and went, but Dors always seemed to be in great debt. She had played Vegas with a twenty-piece orchestra and all the trimmings, but now in Britain and having to earn a living to pay off her debts she was forced to take offers that she perhaps once wouldn't, with the band greatly reduced sometimes to just a two-piece; piano and drums. She hit upon this great idea; in America, Doris

Day would do concerts in Vegas. At the end Rock Hudson would come on with a bunch of flowers and Doris Day would always say, "Ooh what a surprise, it's Rock Hudson." So, at her concerts that's what we did. During the finale, I would come on with a bouquet of flowers and she'd say, "Ooh, Jess Conrad." She'd do this whole schtick, "Ooh, isn't he handsome, ladies?" and things like, "I saw him first!" On the way to these gigs, we'd more often than not be halfway there and Dors would say to me in her wonderful RADA accent, "Oh fuck it, I've forgotten the flowers!" So, we'd stop somewhere, buy the flowers and then continue on our way. Little did the public know that, unlike Doris Day, Dors bought her own flowers!

On one occasion, we arrived in her pink Cadillac and were ushered into the manager's office, which doubled up as the number 1 dressing room. The owner, a little Jewish man, was so thrilled to meet Dors that he had brought his whole family with him; the wife, her mother etc. Surprised to see me, Dors added, "and I've brought my dear friend Jess Conrad with me," and they were obviously all equally thrilled to meet me. Two for the price of one comes to mind! Dors said, "Before I say hello to your beautiful wife, let's get the business done." Now, as I knew what fee she was on, she handed me the traditional brown envelope and said, "Check the readies, Jess," which I did. After giving her the nod, I said, "All in order, Dors," at which point she turned to the manager's wife and put on the charm. In the centre of the office that was doubling up as a dressing room, sat a large flower pot in which a towering tree with all its branches reaching the ceiling and spreading across it. It was rather beautiful. All the manager talked proudly about was his wonderful tree that he'd lovingly nurtured for years. Dors and I both appeared to be interested, but of course we weren't. Eventually, the manager and his family left us there to get ready, and he cordially supplied us with a bottle of champagne to enjoy.

Having relaxed for some time enjoying a few glasses of bubbly, Dors said that she needed to pee. I said to her, "Well, the only place to go is the public toilet, which is down the corridor," to which she said, "I don't pee with the ordinaries!"

So, I asked, "Well, what are you going to do then, darling?" I then noticed her gazing at the flowerpot in the centre of the room, and she turned to me and nodded, "That'll do". Without hesitation, she pulled her gusset to one side and peed in the flowerpot. Having been the coalman's boy and the milkman's boy, I've seen horses peeing but I've never seen anybody piss like Dors did on that day. The ferocity caused stones and mud to fly everywhere. I said, "For fuck's sake, Dors!" as debris from the pot was flying all over my white jacket, "I'm going on stage later!" When she finally finished and put things back in order, she went off and had a mirror check and went on stage. I stood at the back and worked the spotlight and then took the flowers on during the finale to a huge round of applause.

Everything went splendidly until we got back in the office to see that the tree that once stood magnificently proud, growing up the wall and ceiling was now flat on the floor and looking sad and as dead as a dodo. "Oh fuck!" I said, "Your pissing has killed the tree! He'll go berserk when he sees this." Dors, quick as you like, said, "Well, we've got the readies, let's do a Houdini!" So off we went. As we jumped into the car Dors said to me, "And so ends

another fun-packed evening", a statement she used many times over the years, and we laughed all the way back to the Manor. We had so many fun evenings. Whenever we went out together, something funny would always happen that would always amuse us. At the time, all the number one clubs in the West End would have chairs with our names on the back, including *Club dell'Aretusa* in the Kings Road and *Stringfellows*.

The High Priestess was Dors' moniker, as she liked the idea of being the lady leader. She'd call me her 'Man of Bronze', as I always had a suntan. A lot has been documented about Diana Dors' wild parties over the years, with orgies and X-rated antics in the pool. People would hear about Dors' parties and they became legendary. Anybody who attended them would probably be disappointed and embellish stories to make them sound more risqué than they were and, of course, to ensure they were thought of as one of the in-crowd. In truth, the parties were a bit more raucous when Dors was with Dennis Hamilton but considering the things that happen today, they were like Alice in Wonderland. Dors parties were more about mischievous behaviour, playing games like *The Truth Game,* where a small gathering of people would sit around and answer awkward questions. We'd enjoy a few drinks and someone would bring some dope. It was well-known that showbiz people used to indulge in a bit of cannabis, but it was no longer the in-thing when it became a common recreation that everybody was doing. I've always worked hard for my money, so I certainly wouldn't waste it on buying any kind of drug myself but, like Dors, if they're passed around the table, we would of course take a puff. It made Dors giggle a lot and she'd ask questions like, "out of the people here, who would you least like to sleep with and why?" Relaxing, you'd tell the truth and you'd find yourself laughing at things that were only funny because you were slightly high. I remember Dors once laughing hysterically at a man across the room with funny ears. I had to point out that they weren't his ears. He was wearing false ears for a laugh. The type you get from a joke shop.

David Jacobs, the famous disc jockey, having heard the stories of Dors' legendary gatherings, would say to me every time he saw me in the West End, "Put me in, Jess," suggesting I invite him to one. I mentioned it to Dors on several occasions, and every time her reply was that he wasn't her cup of tea. She liked her men with a bit more of a bad boy image. But he kept pestering me every time I saw him. So, finally she gave in, suggesting I invite him to come to one particular lunchtime gathering. She must have had something in mind. When I told him, it was like he'd won the pools. He didn't believe me at first, but I told him to be at The Manor at one o'clock.

When he arrived, I opened the door wearing a dressing gown and told him to get his gear off straight away. He was so excited that he stripped off bollock-naked down to his black patent shoes, socks and suspenders. He asked me excitedly, "What happens now?" to which I replied, "Go through that door, they're waiting for you," and in he went. It was pitch black and he took three or four steps before Dors switched the lights on to reveal a room full of smartly dressed couples and a naked David Jacobs, and announced, "Ladies and Gentlemen, this must be a first. The well-known disc jockey David Jacobs in his birthday suit!"

# 28: Touring South Africa with Kathy Kirby

Kathy Kirby and I were both at London Management being represented by Jean Diamond when they asked me if I'd like to tour South Africa with her. Kathy was a big star then. She had a big hit with her cover version of Doris Day's *Secret Love,* and had represented the United Kingdom in the 1965 *Eurovision Song Contest* where she finished in second place. She was one of the best-known and most-recognised personalities in British showbusiness. Kathy Kirby was an incredible looking woman and bore a resemblance to Marilyn Monroe. She was probably the biggest female star to come out of this country at that time. My god, she was a knockout and looked gorgeous. She was a wonderful lady. Her manager and boyfriend was Bert Ambrose, who was a very shrewd man and directed her in the right way, making sure that the lighting was good, and that she looked good and wore expensive clothes. She looked like a star. She *was* a star. I think the reason why Kathy Kirby was so well-paid was because of Bert Ambrose. He was obviously a good manager and he got her to become the highest-paid performer in Britain.

When we got to South Africa, I found out that Kathy Kirby's musical director was a very good friend of mine who was one of the piano players I used back in England. So, I thought, that's great, he could play for me as well as the South African musicians weren't quite tuned-in to British pop music. It turned out he was very happy to play for me, but when Ambrose found out he put a stop to it. Although I was upset at the time, it did prove that Ambrose was astute and a good manager to her.

Apart from going on stage and doing her forty-five-minute slot, Kathy Kirby was mainly locked in her room. She lived a hermit's life with Ambrose. He was a Svengali figure. She had this belting voice, and it really hit you at the back of the stalls. She really knew how to deliver a song, but I didn't see a lot of joy in her face apart from when she was on stage.

In 1971, when Ambrose died, there was nobody to take that position and she very quickly worked less and less, or didn't work at all, and perhaps started to drink a bit. Years later, I was performing at a theatre in Chesterfield. I was just finishing my sound check when somebody told me Kathy Kirby was also on the bill and would I mind if she used my band. So, I went and knocked on her dressing room door and this lady opened the door, and I thought it was the cleaner. So, I said, "Excuse me, is Kathy there?" This lady said, "Oh don't be silly. It's me you, silly sod!" And it *was* Kathy Kirby. I was shocked as I didn't recognise her. She had deteriorated so much. It's a cruel thing to say, but she didn't look like the same Kathy Kirby.

When we did the rehearsal, I said to her, "I understand you'll be using my band. Where are your parts?" She looked blankly and said, "I haven't got any," as if I was talking Chinese to her. For somebody as famous as Kathy Kirby not to have band parts was quite unbelievable. She had no music, no nothing; and that was only the start of things. Realising the state she was in, the boys said not to worry about it as they'd busk. My piano player said that he would write the parts out for her. We couldn't find any paper and he actually wrote top line to *Secret Love* out on a fag packet.

The night of the show, she came out and was completely incoherent. She didn't seem to know where she was on stage. Things got worse and worse. It was quite unbelievable to see a star of that magnitude acting like she had never been on a stage before. She stopped many times, forgetting the words and blaming the band. It was just like watching Judy Garland. She was all over the place.

Years later, I was interviewed for a TV documentary called *Kathy Kirby, The Golden Girl of Pop* where I recalled touring South Africa with her. Her story is an archetypal showbiz story really. She had it all and lost it all. You have to be surrounded by the right people, don't you? She was used and abused. It was a very sad ending for a great talent like that.

# 29: Bond Audition

Gareth Hunt and I were having a drink after playing charity golf for the Variety Club of Great Britain, as one does, and I said to him by a way of making a profound statement, "Gareth, do you realise, all big movie stars have blue eyes?" and he said, "Like who?"

"Paul Newman", I replied. "Perhaps that's where we're going wrong?" He questioned why I would say such a thing. So I said, "Yeah, but you know, MOVIES… I'll look into it." And I did. I found out that blue contact lenses were available and they were non-prescription. In other words, you look like *The Man from Atlantis* but you can't see anything. Furthermore, they cost an astronomical amount. So, I hit on a great idea of buying a pair and splitting the cost with Gareth. I decided we'd have one eye each! I'd have the right eye, and he'd have the left eye. So if I got an audition, I'd ring him up and he'd bring the left eye over. Or vice versa.

Then, out of the blue, I got an audition to play James Bond. Sean Connery had left and they were looking for a new Bond for *On Her Majesty's Secret Service*. The casting director thought I would be ideal for the part. So I phoned Gareth to ask him to bring the left eye over. Obviously, the first question he asked me was, "what are you auditioning for, Jessie?" I told him it was some funny old commercial, after all I didn't want to tell him it was *Bond* as he would have instantly gone away and got an audition for himself!

On the day of the audition, I arrived in good time at Cubby Broccoli's office, just behind The Dorchester Hotel off Park Lane, only to be told by the Casting Director, "You can go up straight away, Jess." So, I excitedly went up the stairs two at a time, got to Cubby Broccoli's door and hastily knocked on it. I heard a voice inviting me to come in. I was a little out of breath and I couldn't go into the room like that, as that would be very un-Bondish! Also, in my haste, I had forgotten to put my eyes in. So, I quickly put my left eye in and then, realising that Cubby Broccoli was probably staring at the door waiting for me to enter, I panicked and the right contact lens fell onto the

floor. I recovered the lens and hurriedly put it into my right eye only to find that it had a bit of carpet hair lodged in it!

Now I couldn't see a thing. I remembered that when John Wayne walked into a room, he never put his back to the audience and I certainly didn't want to put my back to the powerful movie producer Cubby Broccoli, who was in a position to make me the next James Bond. So I pushed the door open with my right hand, stepped in, closed the door behind me with my left hand, flicked my cuffs and looking straight ahead in typical Bond fashion said, "My Name's Conrad, Jess Conrad". And then I heard a voice saying, "I'm over here!"

Anyway, the role in *On Her Majesty's Secret Service* went to George Lazenby. What a mistake that was!

# 30: Early 1970s – Cool It Carol

By 1970, I was very involved with Diana Dors and what went with it socially. I was making films in quick succession and was the busiest man about town. I was a very popular film actor and the part of Jonathan in *Cool it Carol* could have been written for me, so it would seem. I was a natural choice.

*Cool It Carol* was a cautionary tale of a couple of youngsters who leave the sticks to venture into swinging London in search of fame and fortune but fall into a world of pornography, drugs, and prostitution. Robin Askwith, who played the lead role, was at the time just starting out in the business. We played golf at least once a week together, for the Actor's Golfing Society. We played showbiz football every week and we were out clubbing every

*Lobby card for* Cool It Carol

week. So, that is how close our friendship was. He was probably my best friend at the time as we seemed to do everything together and I was like a big brother to him. I gave Robin Askwith the codename Trick Lips and Squiffy. As Squiffy rolled off the tongue easier, he became known to all the technicians on the film by that name. I, of course, was always called JC.

Squiffy loved to take his clothes off in films. Whereas I always use 'Would Elvis do it?' as my yardstick and therefore didn't. I do not know any other actor in Britain at the time who would be as happy to take his clothes off as Robin Askwith was. Getting naked became his trademark, which has made him the evergreen performer he is today. Pete Murray was also in the film. Pete has always insisted, as our real surnames are both James, that we are somehow related. Pete and I have been friends since we both played for the TV All Stars Football Team, and have played charity golf and remained friends for what seems like forever.

One of the biggest Hollywood character actors at the time was also in the film, Stubby Kaye, who co-starred with Marlon Brando & Jean Simmons in *Guys & Dolls*. Stubby Kaye had come to England to star in *Man of Magic* at the Piccadilly Theatre, ended up falling in love with one of the chorus girls, Angela Bracewell, marrying her and settling here. Stubby Kaye was a great character on and off screen and settled well into the British acting establishment.

I had never worked with the director Pete Walker before, but that was to be an enjoyable experience too. I wore a fur coat in the film, which was acceptable at the time. It was a part that I knew suited me, being not far off the mark from the real Jess Conrad. It was a case of don't act Jess, just *be* Jess. Most of the dialogue was ad-libbed and we had a fabulous time making the movie. One scene involved me seducing the actress Janet Lynn on the billiard table. Ordinarily the director would ask for a closed set as the scene was pretty raunchy. But in this case, word got out that I was doing this erotic scene and it was almost like they were selling tickets just to watch the filming. Pete Walker didn't seem too bothered that the likes of Dors and some other famous people came on set that day to watch. It was such a fun shoot that it became one of the highlights of the movie.

Pete Walker was so into how I behaved that he insisted that I took part in his next film *The Flesh and Blood Show* in 1972 with Jenny Hanley, the daughter of Jimmy Hanley, who was a big star in *Dixon of Dock Green*, and the film star Dinah Sheridan. I bought Bambi Lodge in Denham from them. I received Special Guest Star billing just to have a sex scene with Jenny Hanley. It wasn't much more than a lingering kiss, but I remember Pete Walker

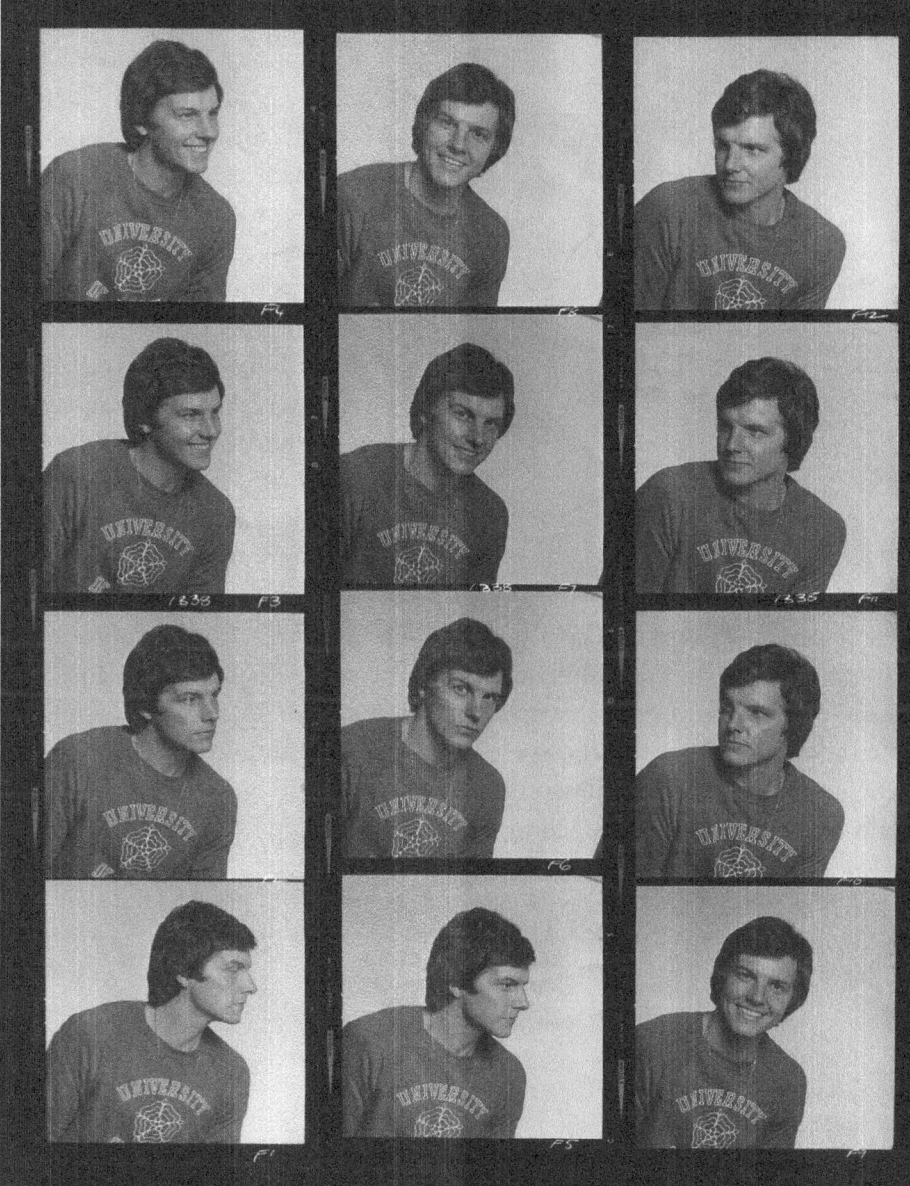

saying it was a masterpiece. I must admit it was quite a long time for two people to be entwined.

I played *Jack and the Beanstalk* at the New Theatre Cardiff in 1970. Earle & Vaughan were in this show along with Joan Mann, Maggie Vickers, and Nicholas Brent as the giant. Joan Mann was another throwback from old-school pantomime, she sang with this big operatic voice and still believed that principal boy should be played by a woman. She was well and truly stuck in the past. This was the first time I met Norman Vaughan, who I got on well with. We had the same sense of humour and loved showbusiness with the same degree of passion. We became bosom buddies and would go on to appear in another couple of pantos together. Opposite the stage door was a famous club, *Tito's*, where all the great acts played. We would see the likes of Frankie Vaughan, Max Bygraves etc play there on a Monday night.

# 31: Godspell

In 1968, I starred in *The Foundations* at the Arts Theatre Club on Great Newport Street and Derek Bowman, who was mentoring a young boy called David Essex, came to see the show and said to me, "He wants to be like you one day." Little did we know then that he would soon go on to have a meteoric rise to fame, rather like I did in the 1960s.

In 1971, David Essex was offered the role of Jesus in *Godspell*. The musical was written by Stephen Schwartz based on a book by John-Michael Tebelak and portrayed Jesus as a clown. The structure of the show was that of a series of parables, based on the Gospel of Matthew. These are then interspersed with a variety of modern music set to lyrics from traditional hymns. It opened at the Roundhouse and later transferred to Wyndham's Theatre.

After a year, when David Essex decided to leave, the producers were struggling to think of somebody with the same background and charisma who could take over the role. Binkie Beaumont, the theatrical impresario who ran H.M. Tennent, remembered me from playing the understudy to Brook Williams, Emlyn Williams' son, in *These People, Those Books* with Sarah Churchill. So, Binkie Beaumont invited me to audition for the lead role. At the audition, I remember being up against the likes of people like Richard O'Sullivan. I got the part.

As soon as I got the role, I went to see the show and realized that having toured in *My Gentleman Pip*, the musical version *of Great Expectations* and played

Macheath, the lead, in *Threepenny Opera* to name but a few, playing the lead in *Godspell* would be well within my capabilities. I went to see David Essex after the show, and we discussed the role. He congratulated me on accepting the role and told me he knew I'd be great in it, as we had many things in common.

The national tour was more successful and took more money than the West End production. It was such a hot-ticket, much like *Phantom* in the 80s, that people used to come from all over the continent to see it. We played the major theatres in every town and, because it was such a success, we tended to play a month in each town as opposed to a week which was standard. I worked with some delightful people, who later went on to be as famous as I was then. The likes of Lesley Joseph and Susie Blake. Playing Jesus in *Godspell* felt like a breath of fresh air. This was the era of the boy-next-door, cockney boys à la David Essex, Tommy Steele, Michael Caine, Adam Faith, and a time when you didn't have to have a RADA accent to be famous. Whereas before, the only chance of becoming successful was if you came from a privileged background with parents who could afford to put you through RADA.

At the time, my daughter Natalie was going to a convent nursery and one morning the nuns were asking the children what their fathers did. Owing to the fact we lived in Denham Village, which is known as an affluent suburb, most of the children would answer, "My father's a bank manager," "My dad's a lawyer," "Mine's a doctor". When asked what her father did, my daughter Natalie replied, "My father is Jesus!"

"Oh Begorrah!" the nun exclaimed in shock horror. The nun then repeated the question saying, "Don't be silly Natalie, what does your father do for a living?" only to get the same answer. On asking the third time, the nun, running out of patience, took a much sterner tone, "Don't be a naughty girl, I'll ask you one more time Natalie, what does your father do for a living?" Not understanding why the nun seemed angry, Natalie gave her the same reply only to get a clip around the ear. The nun immediately called my wife Renée and told her that Natalie was misbehaving. Renée rushed to the nursery to find out what the trouble was, and the nun told her, "Well, when I asked what your husband did for a living. Natalie said that he was Jesus!" Renée said quite calmly, "Yes, well he is Jesus this week. But next week he'll be Prince Charming. He's an actor you see!"

Being a family man, it was very important for me to be able to get home every weekend, which was sometimes a challenge. I remember on a Saturday I would park my car outside the stage door and even have the car pointed in the direction of London for a speedy getaway. On one occasion, when we were playing Edinburgh, I had to decide whether to catch the last train home, which was the sleeper, or to drive. Having done two shows on a Saturday, driving from Edinburgh home would have been a hell of a task, but to catch the sleeper, I had exactly fifteen minutes from curtain down to get to the station. The finale of *Godspell* sees Jesus being crucified on a fence singing, "Oh God I'm bleeding," which was emotionally draining and drew real tears. I've never had as fulfilling a finale in any other musical as this.

Meanwhile, back home, Renée would drive both my daughters to Marylebone and leave the car in an adjacent street with the keys under the tyre, something that nowadays you couldn't even consider, but then didn't seem so risky. They would then get the train back to Denham, leaving the car for me to pick up in the early hours of the next morning.

So there I was, on the second performance on the Saturday Night, having booked a taxi, not to pick me up at the stage door but at the front of the theatre so that I could actually come off the cross, run up the aisle and get straight into it. As opposed to spending half an hour signing autographs at the stage door, which I wouldn't be able to do. After the curtain call, I got out of my costume, got into my day clothes which were stage left in a neat pile in the prompt corner, and sprinted up the aisle. Unfortunately, by the time I got to the taxi I had been spotted, which wasn't difficult being who I am, 6ft 2 and eyes of blue. I thought that I wouldn't be but, I guess, it's impossible not to be. At that point, getting into the taxi was a nightmare as members of the audience obviously wanted my autograph. I was in a panic as my train was leaving in five minutes. The taxi driver got me to the station as fast as he could. I jumped out of the cab, throwing a tenner at him and started this particularly long run down a particularly long platform to get to my sleeper. I made it just in the nick of time and just as the train started to move, I got to my carriage. Once in there, I looked into a mirror which happened to have a crack in it and the face looking back at me was a clown crying, because the Jesus makeup had a tear on both eyes. I was emotionally drained having worked hard all night with the audience loving me, and now here I was looking at myself in my clown's makeup alone, through a cracked mirror, which seemed so poignant and a moment I've never forgotten.

# 32: Even More Panto – 1972 & 1974

1972 saw me starring in *Dick Whittington* again. This time at the Wimbledon Theatre with Jack Douglas, Norman Vaughan, and Dana. At last, I was spending Christmas at home. How wonderful it was to be playing the Wimbledon Theatre which seemed to become my second home over the years. In those days, you could park anywhere which was great, and there was a lovely café opposite the stage door and the dressing rooms were each unique. Today, they look like a concentration camp! But in those days, the theatre manager would bring the female star a bouquet of flowers at the beginning of the run, and the male star a bottle of scotch. Those days are long gone, when the theatre was a very special place to work in.

Jack Douglas, a very fine comic made famous by his funny twitch in *The Carry Ons*, played Idle Jack. Jack became another great friend of mine; he was somebody that knew all the tricks of the trade and used them to his advantage. The thing I could never work out, although he was playing Idle Jack wearing workman's overalls, he also wore an enormous diamond ring. When I asked him why he said, "I'll show you." So, I went and sat in the audience and, sure enough, when he came on stage and the follow spot hit him, the eye was immediately drawn to the glare from this magnificent diamond ring. Yet another lesson in upstaging.

Comedian Norman Vaughan was playing the dame, and he told me that he thought it was a good thing to do because as you get older as an actor, you can still always play the Dame. While we were in rehearsals, he got the call from TV Producers saying that they wanted him to host the ATV gameshow, *The Golden Shot*. Had he got *The Golden Shot* before he was cast as Dame, he most certainly wouldn't have played the role in panto. At that point, he ditched playing the dame with its over-the-top camp mannerisms and instead just walked through the part without any characterization.

Dana, a big name through her success of winning *Eurovision* that year, turned out to be a genuinely nice, wholesome Irish girl with no showbiz affectation. Backstage with my dresser, I asked him whether he knew that Dana was a lesbian. He replied, "You're joking? What do you mean she's a lesbian?"

I said, "Well, she doesn't fancy me."

He said, "Maybe she doesn't like you?".

So I said, "Oh no, don't tell me her eyesight's gone as well!"

1974 saw me back in panto again at Wimbledon, this time in *Goldilocks and the Three Bears*. Whoever's idea it was to do *Goldilocks and the Three Bears*, a pantomime subject that has never worked before at a premier theatre like Wimbledon, was on a hiding to nothing. First, for a panto to work the book has to be well-written and the major problem with Goldilocks is visualising how the three bears are going to work. To do it properly, you need six actors (back legs and front legs) and three good bear costumes, which is enough of an expense before you start thinking about the cost of everything else. I special guest starred as Hank the Yank, and on the first day of rehearsals we read through the script without the help of our star Dick Emery who refused to read the script. Lionel Blair, who was the director, said that the rest of us should take our cue from whatever he should have said. Then after a couple of days, we came to plotting out the moves on the stage, known as walking the show. Once, Dick Emery wouldn't do that, so his roadie did it. I thought to myself, when is he ever going to rehearse this part? The answer was never.

Come opening night, I walked down to the prompt corner just to get my bearings, closely followed by Dick Emery, then in character as Mandy, and the first thing he said to me was, "Ooh you are awful, but I like you," and he certainly did, or rather she certainly did. Dick Emery had then turned into a very amorous woman with wandering hands everywhere. Now, I have been around a long time, but this came as a shock even to me. I know all about method acting, but this was ridiculous. I couldn't believe this was the actor that acted like he didn't like me all through rehearsals and wouldn't rehearse. Now, he was all over me like a woman possessed! So much so, that I left the prompt corner to go backstage and realised that he was following me, so hid in a cupboard and I could hear him say, "Where's that lovely Jess Conrad?" still in character as this octopus-handed woman! That was embarrassing enough, but worse was to come. When the show was finished, he appeared as alter ego Ton Up Boy, the biker character, full monty with leather boots, bikers' scarf etc, as butch as you like, saying in a loud gruff voice, "Let's all go to that Italian restaurant, but don't bring that Jess Conrad along, he'll pull all the birds!" Dick Emery then got onto his motorbike, revving up more than I thought was necessary, making a terrible din, and off he went Marlon Brando-esque à la *Wild One*, up the hill to the Italian restaurant. The panto was not a success and was never done again. I have always admired Dick Emery's talent but would have liked us to become close friends, as was the usual outcome with me doing panto.

# 33: Northern Clubs

It's hard to believe that for many years variety acts went up north to earn a living. That was the way showbiz was then. You would drive back to London with both pockets filled with rolled-up pound notes, it was a wonderful feeling. There were so many working men's clubs, though *Batley Variety Club* was perhaps the most well-known of them all. Stars from America would directly fly into Leeds Airport; the likes of Johnny Ray, Gene Pitney, and The Four Tops to name but a few.

As there were no backing tracks in those days, I had to take my band *The Hollywood Rock Machine* (I thought it was a rather good name at the time) with me. The band, consisting of the likes of Mac Poole or Clem Cattini on drums, would meet at my house, put the gear into Mac's transit van, and off we'd go. The booking agents were pretty much always based up north and well-known for being quite slippery characters. Many times I went to the so-called office to collect our money on a Saturday, only to find an empty office, or worse still no office at all. No man, no money. Having been duped on occasion, if a new booking came in, you'd have to ring around other acts and find out if a promoter was kosher or not. After a while, you'd learn to only work for promoters that you've worked with before.

The contracts were always stated as two shows a day, and we'd be hired for a whole week. The big clubs like Batley Variety or Stockton Fiesta were the ones that paid the big money, but because we agreed to do two shows a day and we were now at the disposal of the promoter all week, he could put us into anywhere he liked for the first. So, on paper, it looked like a good deal, except the first venue of the day was always a place where they wouldn't normally see named-acts. So we'd often get sent to places for next to nothing, and they'd be the most undesirable venues. Like a pub on a Monday night who maybe have never hosted a show before, but would probably only be paying a token fee and couldn't believe they had a big star like Jess Conrad or many others who were big names at the time like John Leyton, Mark Wynter, Billie Davis, or Wee Willie Harris. I remember, on many occasions,

climbing flights of stairs with an amp under my arm to help out the band. It was common practice in the smaller venues who weren't used to having big stars to prove that one was appearing. So, in the front of house, they'd actually display my signed contract for everyone to see, which included the fee, which most ordinary people wouldn't earn in a year, but of course did include the fee for the entire band as well as myself. So the audience would have the right hump with you before you even came on stage, which made playing these clubs even more challenging than it was anyway.

The other downside was that in some of these smaller clubs, the rock 'n' roll revolution was new to them. They would never before have had girls screaming at the local boy who got up to sing. Whereas when I got up, they screamed all the way throughout. I once had an in-depth chat, one pop star to another, with Gene Pitney. I told him I was always worried about not remembering the words to the songs. To which he replied, "When you're a sex symbol like you are, the volume of the screaming teenagers means that nobody hears what you're singing anyway!"

I remember doing a club, which was the first show of the day and this sort of thing happened more often than not, I would go on and there was a wall of sound of girls screaming. That's what I'm used to. But the club owner, having never experienced anything like this before, switched my mic off and said to the audience, "Order. Order. If you don't settle down, I'll take the turn off." The audience didn't know what's happening, and by now they've missed half of the song. I am so pissed off, with a four-piece live band, trying to do my show. The next thing I know, the club owner turns the mic off again to announce, "The pie man's come," at which point the whole audience disperse to the back of the room to get their pies. Even if it had been Elvis Presley they would have done the same. You can't compete with the pie man up north!

There were so many of us up north. After I'd finished my show, I went to Batley Variety Club to see Bob Monkhouse, who Diana Dors always had a secret crush on. Bob had two acts, the squeaky clean gameshow host à la *The Golden Shot* and the risqué Northern club act, which was unbelievably blue. After the show, I went to his dressing room and his opening line was, "Congratulations on your first wrinkle." Horrified at the remark, I had a quick mirror check to make sure I was still perfect. Bob was in fits of laughter that I'd fallen for his quip.

## 34: Persona

I'm unique in that I've had two careers; I was a budding actor having spent two years in rep learning my trade for tuppence a week and then overnight because I was lucky to be cast as a pop star in the *Play of the Week*, I was voted England's Most Popular Singer in 1961 over Cliff Richard, Adam Faith, Marty Wilde etc.

A Souvenir of an evening spent with JESS CONRAD

Be-bop-a-lula
Dizzy Miss Lizzie etc...

It was then thrust upon me to be a popstar, and as my father was a singer in a jazz band, it seemed second nature to me. But I didn't want to be an Elvis clone, I wanted to be my own unique character. I have never shied away from a mirror, and whenever I would naturally look in one I was quite pleased, and people would laugh. But instead of them laughing at me, I wanted them to laugh with me. So gradually, over time, I started to develop a persona, and before long that persona would actually become my real self.

At a very young age I realized that being good looking could be used to your advantage by making it humorous. I remember a wrestler called

Gorgeous George who would come into the ring, all in pink, carrying a silver mirror while spreading rose petals at his feet. Another influence was a young Liberace, who was outrageously dressed and humorous.

I've always been a natural show-off. People hated me at first sight because of my good looks. When you're a beautiful person, they love to hate you. So, you can't win. So you try and send up your good looks by taking the nobble off it. My friend and neighbour Roger Moore had it down to a fine art. Yes, I'm beautiful, but I don't take myself that seriously. So, that is what I thought my image could be. The trouble was it worked very well for the variety side of my career, the light entertainment side, but when it came to the acting it made people look upon me as more lightweight, as opposed to being serious. So, I was caught between a rock and a hard place. In fact, it has been a problem throughout my life. If you're the best-looking boy at twelve, you're going to be the best looking at eighty-five. Nothing's changed. You've got to over-act by being nice to people because they're looking for you to fail.

That said, I have used the persona to my advantage in my cabaret. Here's a little taster:

Good evening, ladies and gentlemen, my name's Jess Conrad. What's my name? [audience: Jess Conrad] Thank you, fans. I mention that because, to tell you the truth, I just adore the sound of my own name. No, I mention that because a lot of people think I'm his son. No, I know it sounds like a joke but it's perfectly true. When I arrived at The London Palladium earlier today, I was in the foyer when a woman my age – well not my age, nobody's my age except Victor Mature, and he's dead! She said, "Are you the real Jess Conrad? Or are you a tribute?" and she looked at me as though I was an antique table! And just for a joke, you know, being Jack the Lad I said, "No, actually I'm his son". She said, "You are Jess aren't you?" because she caught the twinkle. Ding. She went all peculiar. She said, "Ooh Jess," she said, "Ooh Jess," she said. "Well, you know, Jess I used to have your picture on my bedroom wall," I said, "I still have". She said, "You don't understand Jess. I'm his greatest fan". I said, "No you're not…" [audience: I am!] She said, "Will you sign this autograph?" I said, "Who shall I sign it for?" She said, "Sign it to Jess, I named my son after you". I said, "How old is the little tot?" She said, "Next Thursday he'll be fifty-eight!" When I sing people scream, but I won't stop. And women throw things! Now they used to be quite small but now they're effing humongous. This is fantastic I wish I was out front watching this.

Some more Jess one-liners are on the next page...

» My fans fall for me, mainly because they're too old to stand up.

» I'm the only person that walks down lover's lane holding his own hand.

» A lot of these sixties stars sell their memorabilia in the foyer after the show, but I think that's rather crass. But I do have a lovely line in homemade strawberry jam.

» [walking downstage] Excuse my back, but then again, my back is better than most men's fronts.

» It's great to be here. I thought they'd send a car. They sent a map.

» It's my father I have to thank for my good looks. He's a plastic surgeon.

» [Looking at the front row] There's Fifty Shades of Grey in this one row alone.

» I'm still attractive to women. Two were fighting over me the other night. So, I had to phone the police. They said, "What's wrong?" I said, "The fat one's winning!"

» I was in bed with a woman the other night, she said, "You're well endowed". I said, "You're pulling my leg!"

» For those of you who haven't seen me since the 1960s on a black and white television, you must be so thrilled to see me in colour.

» Do you like the suit? Gee I'm thrilled. You bought it.

» Hands up all the survivors from the 60s. The 60s, when a blow job meant a Tony Curtis haircut. Naughty, naughty Jess. Naughty but nice.

» I'm not a bad man. How could I be with a face like this?

» I'm going to put you in a dank, dark, horrible place. The front row of one of my concerts.

» I'm going to stay in showbiz, until I'm the only one left.

» And for my headstone: "Here lies Jess Conrad. Nobody loved him more than he loved himself".

# 35: Space 1999

In 1975, I auditioned to play the part of Tony Verdeschi, the juvenile lead in Gerry Anderson's *Space 1999*. At the film test, I remember the casting director liking me a great deal. In the end, they decided to use an all-American cast and hired Tony Anholt instead. But I must have impressed them as they invited me to Guest Star in one of the episodes, *The Lambda Factor*. It was one of the very few times I got to play a character that had nothing to do with being a pop star. So, it was purely on my acting talent that I got the part.

Once again, I have to say how forward-thinking I was to have bought my house in Denham as I could get to Pinewood Studios in five minutes from there. By that time, I had got used to working with famous actors, but when I was told that I was going to be playing opposite Martin Landau, I remember wondering, the day before filming, what one would talk about to an archetypal Hollywood legend.

By this time, I had made so many films that I did start to engage with my fellow actors more. You cannot very well say things like, "Didn't Arsenal do well last Saturday?" or talk about Coronation Street can you? But I needn't have worried because, in fact, he came over to me, introduced himself, sat down and said, "What size shoes do you take?" I thought, for a Hollywood star to open with a conversation like that was beyond weird! When I replied, "Eleven, and you know what they say about men with big feet?" And jokingly added, "And these are tight!" He then immediately called his wife Barbara Bain over, who was also starring in the series, and said, "Darling, this is Jess Conrad. And look at the size of his feet!" as he started to perspire. As an opening conversation, I would say it must be up there with the most macabre.

The story of *The Lambda Factor* involved Lambda waves permeating Moonbase Alpha causing various instruments to malfunction and people to behave out of character. Crew member Sally dies in mysterious circumstances, I come on the scene as Mark Sanders. The episode was directed by Charles

*Catherine Schell doing my barnet*

Crichton who directed *The Lavender Hill Mob*. He was the only director up until that point to give me a note, which was that I tended to drop my voice on the last word of a sentence. That was helpful for me to know as it was not something I was aware of previously.

I already knew Catherine Schell from working with her on the movie I made in Czechoslovakia, *Hell is Empty*. Although we never shared a scene in this episode, the publicity people made sure there were lots of pictures of us taken together.

I have always made sure that my costumes would show off my physique, and I had my outfit for *Space 1999* specially tailored for me, as I always did. I didn't go to the gym for nothing and wouldn't imagine any other guest star going into so much detail of what he physically looked like. I made sure that my death scene lasted longer than the director could have anticipated. As I have said before, I always want to make a dramatic entrance and a dramatic exit. I realised the way I choreographed it; the scene wouldn't end until I reached the floor dead. So, I acted my socks off and milked it.

After the episode was filmed, Martin Landau took me to a show in the West End which he boasted he had seen more than a dozen times. The opening scene included an actor marching across the stage in large, hobnail boots. It then dawned on me that he must have had a foot fetish.

I am constantly reminded of this job all the time, as the show is always being repeated on television. The show is such a cult hit that there are even collectors' cards containing my image as guest star in *The Lambda Factor* changing hands for hundreds of pounds online.

# 36: Crossroads

In 1978, I was a special guest star in one of the most iconic TV shows of all time, *Crossroads*. My agent at the time, Michael Summerton, also looked after Noele Gordon and before the show started the publicity people got a lot of mileage about the fact that I was going to star opposite her. Noele Gordon was an enormous star then. It was, in their words, like two icons working together, although I never actually shared a scene with her.

I had been a special guest in many TV series, but never a soap opera. On my arrival at the ATV Studios in Birmingham, I was the first to arrive as I always seem to be. I went into the green room where there was a row of empty chairs. I sat on the first one, and I was hastily told that it was Noele's chair. So, I sat in the next one and was told that it belonged to one of the other regulars. This went on until I was sitting in the kitchen on a chair that was short of a leg or two! I thought to myself, this can't be the guest star's chair?!

I played Philip Bailey, who was suspected of killing his wife. When all the actors arrived I was introduced to the actor Charles Morgan who would be playing the coroner, who promptly told me how wonderful it must be for me, being a pop star, to be playing an acting part in this iconic series. I got so bored with this archetypal, pompous, bit-part actor telling me how lucky I was. During a dramatic inquest scene, I realised this actor was hesitant over one particular line, "Whose body was it?" During the take, instead of saying, "Whose body was it?" he said, "Whose bozzy was it?" As he'd previously done his best to put me in my place, I said without hesitation, "Excuse me, coroner, what did you say?" At that moment, the director in the box couldn't have believed what he was seeing and hearing, as this was being shot 'as live'. He probably said to the script supervisor in panic mode, "He's only questioning the coroner!" The coroner then said with clenched fists, while the perspiration was running down his forehead, "Whose… body… was it?" over-emphasising each word. To which I replied, "Oh sorry, coroner, I thought you said, "Whose bozzy was it?" The director must have been having a heart attack! It put a wry smile on my face because during the filming it was him who fucked up, not me.

Now, I have never been the type of actor that goes to the pub every lunchtime and comes back half-cut. I always prefer to use the time to check the script and go through notes that we had received that morning. So, while everyone else was at lunch one day, after I'd finished looking at my script and eaten my sandwich, I was sitting there twiddling my thumbs and had remembered that one of the sparks had told me that there was a striptease parlour three doors down. I wondered if it was true, so I looked out of the window and craned my neck to the right. I saw a glass roof and thought I could probably get a better view if I got out of the window and shimmied along the ledge. Before I could let any reason set in, I was on my way and gazing at these beautiful naked women. I totally lost track of time and realised that I needed to get back. So, I tentatively manoeuvred myself back along the ledge, which I must say was extremely dangerous, but at my age then it didn't bother me. By this time, the cast had returned from the lunch break and reassembled back in the rehearsal room. Suddenly, they saw their guest star shuffling along the window ledge, looking more like Spider-Man than an actor trying to get back into the rehearsal room! With my nose pressed up against the window, one of the actresses, noticing my distress, let me in. The director rather sarcastically said, "Where do you think you've

been, Mr Conrad?" I replied, "I've been having a blimp," which caused the younger members of the cast to laugh, as they realised what I meant.

I enjoyed playing Philip Bailey. To have the last words in an episode of *Crossroads* while the haunting theme tune played, written by the one and only Tony Hatch, was an iconic moment, something I didn't fully appreciate at the time.

# 37: 1978 Panto

1978 saw me doing *Jack & the Beanstalk* in panto at The Watersmeet in Rickmansworth with an incredible cast including Kenneth Connor, Peter Byrne, Cardew Robinson, Derek Roy, and Arnold Ridley from *Dad's Army*. What a joy to be working for the first time in panto within half an hour of where I lived in Denham. I became very friendly with Kenneth Connor.

Peter Byrne, being a good-looking leading man, was worried that I might try and seduce his girlfriend Caroline Ellis. I had no idea she was his girlfriend, and anyway, when I am working on a panto, my thing is not trying to get in bed with the leading lady, especially if she is a member of the cast's girlfriend. It always surprises me that some leading actors are so insecure when I am in the show and it also involves their girlfriend. Cardew Robinson was a huge name, and Derek Roy was a big name in the 1950s, and he was playing Dame for the first time. Arnold Ridley from Dad's Army insisted on calling the giant everything but the giant. For example, "the beast", "the giant monkey", "the gorilla", "King Kong" etc. He could not get it into his head to call the antagonist the giant, which I found very odd as he seemed to remember all the other lines.

All the males in the cast, and this cast was male-heavy, were in one large dressing room and we all got on very well. I remember Derek Roy, while putting on his stockings as Dame, telling me one night that he thought his wife was having an affair. He told me this story in such a manly manner while dressed as a woman and halfway through stopped to ask me whether the seam in his stocking was straight. He explained to me in no uncertain terms he planned to miss the curtain call that night and catch his wife at it with her lover, and then give the guy a good hiding. I thought to myself, hopefully not wearing his high heels!

During this panto, director Julien Temple cast me in *The Great Rock 'n' Roll Swindle*, a film based on the life of the British Punk Rock Band *The Sex Pistols* and their manager Malcolm McLaren. *The Great Rock 'n' Roll Swindle* was to star The Sex Pistols and an array of special guests, of which I was one.

It was agreed with the film producers that I could only shoot in the morning as I had the panto matinee to do.

I was told that I would receive the script on arrival. When I arrived at the location, which was an old Granada Cinema now in disrepair, I wandered around for some time looking for somebody that might be able to help me and finally found the third assistant. I told him who I was, and he led me to a room where I noticed what I thought was a tramp asleep in a chair. So, I sat there twiddling my thumbs while the tramp lay there snoring. After some time, the third assistant returned and I said to him, "Look, can somebody tell me what's going on? I'm Guest Starring in this film, and I need to see a script." He then went off again for some time, only to return with three or four pages of dialogue. I once remember being on a night out with Dors at Tramp Nightclub, and I reminded her that she was doing a scene with Richard Burton the next day. Personally, I would have been at home learning the script. Dors then opened her handbag, glanced at the page of script briefly and said, "Right, that's OK. I've got it." The likes of Jim Davidson and Bobby Davro, who I went on to work with, also had photographic memories, but always dismissed that fact. I didn't have a photographic memory and was certainly going to be hard put to learn all that dialogue in such a short time. I was eventually called upon to follow the third assistant to where we were going to film, which was the auditorium of this broken-down Granada cinema. He sat me next to the infamous pornographic actress Mary Millington, who immediately dumped her handbag on my lap and said, "Hang on to that Jess," as she went off to the loo. The handbag was open, because it couldn't be closed, as it was over-stuffed with five and ten-pound notes.

The ice-cream lady was being played by Irene Handl, one of our best-loved comedy actresses, who years later I would co-star with in panto in Lewisham. When we started filming my scene, I realised that the tramp I was sharing the so-called dressing room with, was in fact the star of the film, Johnny Rotten. When the director shouted "action" through his megaphone, Rotten spewed rubbish. He did not utter one word from the script. At the end of this nonsensical version of the script, he received a round of applause from the assembled crew. I then stood up and said, "Just a minute... He hadn't said one word that was in the written script, yet you all gave him a round of applause? Why was that?" And the director said, "That's as close as he'll ever get." So, on my cue for action, as I wasn't too sure of the script myself, I thought what's good for the goose is good for the gander. So off I went with my version of my own made-up funny bunny. I smiled and generally took the piss, after which I also got a round of applause.

Later, back in the dressing room, the man I believed to be Johnny Rotten's roadie, a big lad, and that's understating the fact, walked in with a heap of white powder piled on the back of his hand and said, "Johnny likes you, mate. He's asked me to give you this," presenting it to me as if he was offering me something special. At which point, he stuck it under my nose. Knowing what it was, I immediately said, "I can't take that mate, I'm playing Jack in Jack & The Beanstalk. I've got a matinee at 2:30." At which point, the burly man said, "Never mind that, cop for this otherwise Johnny will be very upset." I then realised, it wouldn't be Johnny who would be upset, it would be him, and I couldn't really argue with him. He then said that, "Johnny likes Irene Handl as well, and she's just stuffed hers up her nose! And it hasn't affected her." So I followed suit, hoping that by the time I got to the theatre, it would have worn off. How I got to the theatre, I am not sure. But I obviously broke every speed record there is to break. As you can imagine, I was in a right two and eight. Instead of the giant chasing me, I chased the giant up the beanstalk! The whole thing was a nightmare from start to finish. Thank God it was a matinee, and thank God I wasn't reported to the powers that be and I managed to get away with it – just.

# 38: Joseph and the Amazing Technicolor Dreamcoat

I don't want to belittle myself, or overrate myself, but it seemed at the time that the powers that be discovered that as opposed to lots of star names who wouldn't tour the provinces, Jess Conrad would. In the late 70s, theatre managers and promoters realised that *Joseph* was just as successful as pantomime and also could be done any time of the year. So, when I was offered the part of Joseph, I played number one theatres in places like Brighton, Norwich, and Swindon, along with many others. Having played Jesus in *Godspell* and now Joseph, it was such a gift to promoters, and audiences lapped it up.

Bill Kenwright
cordially invites you to
the First Night
of

**JOSEPH**
and the Amazing
**TECHNICOLOR**
**DREAMCOAT**

and to
A PARTY
following the
performance,
to be held
at

*Stringfellows*

UPPER ST. MARTIN'S LANE
LONDON WC2
on
Monday December 15th, 1980.

R.S.V.P.
**BILL KENWRIGHT PRODUCTIONS**
405 STRAND LONDON WC2
TELEPHONE: 01-836 2613/4. 01-836 3793

*Joseph and the Amazing Technicolor Dreamcoat* is based on the story of Joseph from the Bible's Book of Genesis. By now, *Joseph* had been knocking around for over ten years in various incarnations without making any great waves. Although the show was doing good business, the promoter at the time was in financial difficulty over bad deals done in the past, so much so that he couldn't afford to pay the children who were probably only a pound a pop. He was in such a two

and eight that he invited other promoters to see the show in the hope that somebody would take it over. When Bill Kenwright came to see it, he saw the potential right away, and who could blame him? There I was a bona fide top-of-the-bill name who was prepared to tour. I always got rave reviews and, at the time, I was at the peak of my physical fitness. To all intents and purposes, I was the perfect Joseph. So, I was thrilled when Bill took the show on and suggested I carry on playing Joseph.

Bill invited me to his office and told me he was going to tour it starting with Easter Season in Cardiff. Little did we know then that two weeks would become years of successful touring. Bill gave me carte blanche on who I wanted in the show so, naturally, I used all the same people who had been successful with me in the previous run. If it ain't broke, don't fix it comes to mind, as we had all become a very close-knit family. In addition to the number one dressing room, Bill arranged for me to have the adjacent room for all my gym equipment. My gym was such a priority, it even went onto the lorry on a Saturday night before the scenery did. Bill instructed the company manager Jon Swain to look after me and I was very well looked after, as were the rest of the cast. The designer David Terry made sure that my costumes were perfect. My working costume was figure-hugging white dungarees with 'Jo' emblazoned on the chest, and white plimsolls. My loincloth for the prison sequence when I sing 'Close Every Door to Me', one of the highlights of the show, was tailor-made to compliment my physique. Although it was 'poor Joseph' costume, it didn't look unattractive. On the other hand, my transformation into the King of Egypt meant that when I transferred into the Dreamcoat, David pulled out all the stops with a magnificently eye-catching coat of many colours with gold trousers, boots, and a luxurious gold belt which amply showed off my very slim waist. The costume was completed with a diamond-cut medallion necklace and two ruby red rings adorning each little finger, which was enough to get a standing ovation by itself!

Originally the narrator was played by a male actor, who would have to have an outstanding voice as he narrates the story throughout. On occasion, critics would compare our voices and say that the narrator sang beautifully and Jess Conrad acted wonderfully. On observing that comparisons were being made between the two voices, I hit upon the idea of introducing a female narrator. I went to Bill and suggested that it would do the production great service if we changed the narrator to a woman as it was already pretty much a male-dominated show, other than two under-used chorus girls. I also felt that it would appeal to the dads in the audience too. Bill agreed, and it was a remarkable success, and something which Andrew Lloyd Webber could have thanked me for as it is a tradition which still continues to this day.

The cast tended to stay with the production for years and years and that was one of the show's great calling cards. As towns, villages and cities got used to seeing their old friends in the cast time and time again. One of the brothers Benjamin, played by John Melvin, always tried to stand in my follow spot. So, he was nicknamed The Moth, as moths love light! When new brothers came in, they'd anxiously ask John, "What's Jess like?" He would reply, "He's terrific, but he won't call you by your real name, you will have a codename, as we all do." At one point, this new brother came in and was slightly plumpish. After a while, he asked The Moth excitedly, "What is *my* codename?" hoping it would be something quite affectionate, to which The Moth reticently replied, "Unfortunately, your codename is The Blancmange!" One of the brothers, Henry Metcalfe, codename Spider-Man, who was also the choreographer, was so protective of me. One day, he was rehearsing yet another new brother, who at one point accidentally walked in front of me. Henry immediately stopped him and told him in no uncertain terms, "Nobody walks in front of Joseph!" Of all the brothers used, which must have been a hundred, none of them ever achieved stardom. Though it must be noted that Mickie Driver, codename Mother, continues to work to this day in his own old-time musical show wearing a pearly suit. John Melvin, who played Benjamin, stayed with the show throughout its run, and later became a well-known agent, founding the West End agency Principal Artistes.

We were all a tight-knit community, we even had our own newspaper, *The Technicolor Times*. I was codenamed The General and my dressing room was known as HQ, headquarters. I never ever went into the brothers' dressing room, but if ever there was a problem the brothers would go to Jacob, played by Peter Lawrence, codename Matron, and he would report to me. He would also report to Bill Kenwright if there were any problems that needed solving. Most brothers had specific jobs; one would find out where the local gym was, another would find out what was on at the cinema on a Thursday (I'd be doing Radio on a Tuesday and Wednesday was matinee day), and another brother would find a restaurant for us to all eat in on a Friday night, ideally somewhere with a private dining room. We had a five-a-side football team called *The Dreamcoats*, which was made up of me in goal; the same position I played for the Showbiz XI, because I got to wear a different colour costume to everybody else. The team included one of the brothers who was a great footballer, Dave Mayberry who played Pharaoh,

*Celebrating at Stringfellows*

codename The Fonz after Henry Winkler in *Happy Days*, a very popular show at the time, the bass player, and Keith Hayman the Musical Director. Keith was an exceptional MD and would often do midnight matinees with me in concert, which of course Bill gave the theatre manager permission to do. Keith would later go on to become Cliff Richard's musical director. Even Bill Kenwright made guest appearances in the five-a-side team, proving he was not only a theatrical giant and latterly director of Everton football Club, but also a fine footballer in his own right.

The children were a very important part of the show because they sang throughout. On a Monday, while the local children were rehearsing, one of the most difficult things I had to do was to choose one of them to carry on during my first entrance, which made a lovely start to the show. It was important that I chose a child with a naturally smiley or cheeky face, but inevitably there would be some tears from the children who weren't picked. The other difficulty was that their mothers would often want to bring me gifts, which mainly consisted of homemade cakes, and they would insist on delivering them to me personally in my dressing room. The only issue was, more often than not, they wanted to give me more than just the cake!

We played places as far afield as Kirkcaldy, Guildford, and Cardiff. One of the finest managers of that era was Dick Condron in Norwich who would always meet the audience as they went into the theatre, which I thought was a wonderful touch, and he was the only one that did that. I found a whole new legion of fans when I played Joseph. The mothers who had been my original fans in the 1960s when I was a pop star brought their daughters who, after seeing me, would then go on to become my new fans.

The tour was a tremendous success, artistically, financially, and all things showbiz for everybody involved. At the time, my wife Renée was promoting Camay soap (hence her codename Miss Camay) with the legendary Katie Boyle, and they became great friends. On one occasion, Katie asked Renée what I was up to and Renée told her that I was doing a national tour of *Joseph*. Katie asked naively when it was coming to the West End so that she could go and see it. Renée said that it was a touring show and therefore wouldn't be coming to the West End. So, Katie said, "We'll see about that," and had a word with her husband, Sir Peter Saunders, a theatre impresario who owned The Vaudeville Theatre on The Strand. Fortuitously, he had a four-week gap which he needed to fill and so he had a word with Bill Kenwright, and before we knew it, Joseph was in the West End. It was all down to Renée's friendship with Katie Boyle. Talk about 'it's not what you know, but who you' comes to mind!

We enjoyed a very successful run at The Vaudeville which meant I got to sleep in my own bed every night – what joy. Now I was finally in the West End, Bill made sure that my marquee billing was as big as the show title. One day, I got on a bus to go past the theatre just so I could see my name in lights for the first time in the West End, and I was thrilled. Sitting in front of me on the bus were two ladies of a certain age who, just as we were passing the theatre, noticed the poster. One turned the other and said, "Ooh look, Jess Conrad. I wonder if Jess Conrad's his real name," and her friend replied, "Is Jess Conrad *whose* real name?"

The first night that we opened at The Vaudeville, Peter Stringfellow wanted to celebrate the show coming into the West End by throwing a lavish showbiz soiree at his world-famous club. Other than *Tramp* in Jermyn Street at the time, *Stringfellows* was the place to be seen. The party was full of *Joseph* cast members and crew, *Stringfellows* members and celebrities like Chris Quinten, codename Rollerball, who was a regular in Coronation Street, heartthrob stunt driver Eddie Kidd, Lionel Bart, Barry Mason, the man who made Tom Jones a star with the number 1 hit *Delilah*, and socialite Sally Farmiloe, all of whom at the time were showbiz royalty.

We had a short break after our successful run in the West End, only to receive the great news that Bill had negotiated a short season at the world-famous Grand Theatre in Blackpool, which was designed by Frank Matcham. Due to sell-out sales, the run was continually extended. It turned out to be the happiest season I had ever experienced. Our competition on one pier was Bernie Winters with Schnorbitz, as by that time he had split up from his brother Mike, and on the other pier was Russ Abbot. We broke all box office records. If you are a hit in Blackpool, it's rather like being a hit in Vegas. You are the king of the castle. Saturdays were glorious, as not only was I travelling home after the second show, but I always managed to cram in a visit to see Blackpool FC play, as a guest of the management. My family had a wonderful time coming up to visit in the school holidays and we stayed in the headmaster's bungalow at Rossall, the famous boys' school, while the students were on their summer break. We had complete run of the place, which included a full-size swimming pool. My Great Dane, Blue, had a wonderful time chasing the hedgehogs and playing football with them! Les Dawson, the local star comic, seemed to be a fixture in my dressing room as, more often than not, he was waiting backstage to invite me out for drinks. His wife and daughters were also big fans and saw the show on numerous occasions. *Joseph* was extended at least three times. I wasn't sure where we were going after Blackpool, but every week the company manager Jon Swain would put up the touring schedule for the next four weeks on the notice board in the corridor, although of course he would have known the future dates long before that. At no time during the run did I ever contemplate leaving the show, but when I saw the noticeboard with the forthcoming dates, I was shocked to see they were all in Scotland. By this time, I had been in the show for two years and having done the best dates Blackpool, The Vaudeville & Sadler's Wells and I wanted to go out on a high. So, I made a snap decision there and then that I'd had enough of touring. It felt as though I'd been away from home for an eternity and career-wise it seemed to be the right choice. I didn't want to end up like David Whitfield, the famous ballad singer who always seemed to be on the road.

It is hard to believe, but I had no contract with Bill, just a gentleman's agreement. So, when I told Bill I was finished, he was obviously terribly upset, as was I. But all good things must come to an end. It had been a winning combination, he as producer and me as the archetypal Joseph, in a wonderful vehicle. But there comes a time when you have to walk. So, I kind of slipped out without any big fanfare. Theatrically though, I ended on a high at Blackpool, the Vegas of England and, of course, on Joseph's success, I was offered endless tours afterwards, but I decided then that unless it was a contract to say 'pre-West End' that I wouldn't tour again other than my hugely popular one-night stands, *Jess Conrad in Concert*. So, I went on to continue my life as an actor both on stage and screen. Bill was later quoted as saying I made him his first million.

# 39: The Krays

In the late 1970s, Dors rang me up and said, "Ron wants to see you."

I said, "Ron who?"

She said, "Ronnie Kray."

I said, "No Dors, I don't fancy that."

She said, "You can't say no to Ronnie Kray!" By this time Ronnie & Reggie Kray were serving a life sentence at Broadmoor for the murder of Jack "The Hat" McVitie, a book master's clerk, and George Cornell. A man called Joey Pyle, who I later found out was a notorious gangster himself, called me up and introduced himself. He invited me to dinner at the in-place, *Joe Allen's* in Covent Garden, and he made all the right moves. It was obvious that he was taking his orders from Ronnie. He did everything meticulously and ensured I was treated like royalty. I was wined and dined, after which he explained that he'd pick me up and take me to Broadmoor to see Ronnie.

A week later, I arrived at Broadmoor in Joey Pyle's car. I expected to be ushered into a prison cell, instead I was led into a room and there was Ronnie. He was obviously pleased to see me. He spoke very slowly, "Would… you… like… a… cup… of… tea?" like he had all the time in the world to talk. Then he told me that I was still looking good. He complimented me on my great body and asked if I went running. I told him that I did, and then I asked him if he did. He said he did. I looked out the window and said, "Out there on that grass around the courtyard?" and he said, "No, around this room," and I realised I'd put my foot in it.

Then he told me the reason he had asked me to see him. There was a change in his demeanour as he told me that he wanted me to do a show for him.

I thought to myself, *this isn't going to work; I wear a white catsuit, glam rock boots, a jock strap with my wedding tackle well on display and loads of medallions… it's an act for women!* At which point, the tone changed as Ronnie leant forward and told me in no uncertain terms, "Money is no object," as if to say there's no way you can say no to this.

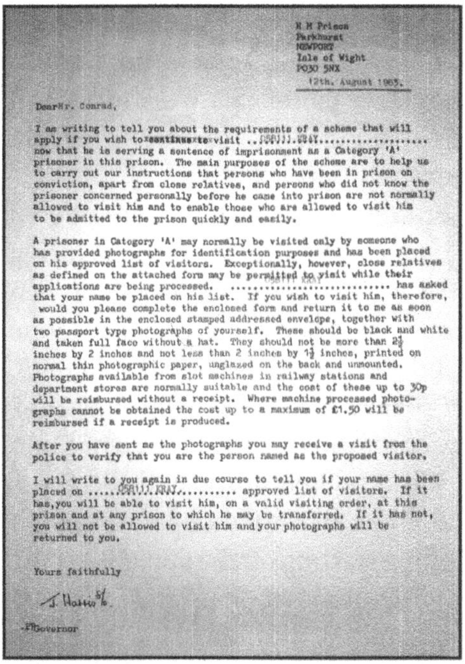

H.M. Prison
Parkhurst
NEWPORT
Isle of Wight
PO30 5NX

12th. August 1963.

Dear Mr. Conrad,

I am writing to tell you about the requirements of a scheme that will apply if you wish to continue to visit ...RONNIE KRAY.................... now that he is serving a sentence of imprisonment as a Category 'A' prisoner in this prison. The main purposes of the scheme are to help us to carry out our instructions that persons who have been in prison on conviction, apart from close relatives, and persons who did not know the prisoner concerned personally before he came into prison are not normally allowed to visit him and to enable those who are allowed to visit him to be admitted to the prison quickly and easily.

A prisoner in Category 'A' may normally be visited only by someone who has provided photographs for identification purposes and has been placed on his approved list of visitors. Exceptionally, however, close relatives as defined on the attached form may be permitted to visit while their applications are being processed. ............................ has asked that your name be placed on his list. If you wish to visit him, therefore, would you please complete the enclosed form and return it to me as soon as possible in the enclosed stamped addressed envelope, together with two passport type photographs of yourself. These should be black and white and taken full face without a hat. They should not be more than 2½ inches by 2 inches and not less than 2 inches by 1½ inches, printed on normal thin photographic paper, unglazed on the back and unmounted. Photographs available from slot machines in railway stations and department stores are normally suitable and the cost of these up to 30p will be reimbursed without a receipt. Where machine processed photographs cannot be obtained the cost up to a maximum of £1.50 will be reimbursed if a receipt is produced.

After you have sent me the photographs you may receive a visit from the police to verify that you are the person named as the proposed visitor.

I will write to you again in due course to tell you if your name has been placed on .....RONNIE KRAY.......... approved list of visitors. If it has not, you will be able to visit him, on a valid visiting order, at this prison and at any prison to which he may be transferred. If it has not, you will not be allowed to visit him and your photographs will be returned to you.

Yours faithfully

J. Harris

Governor

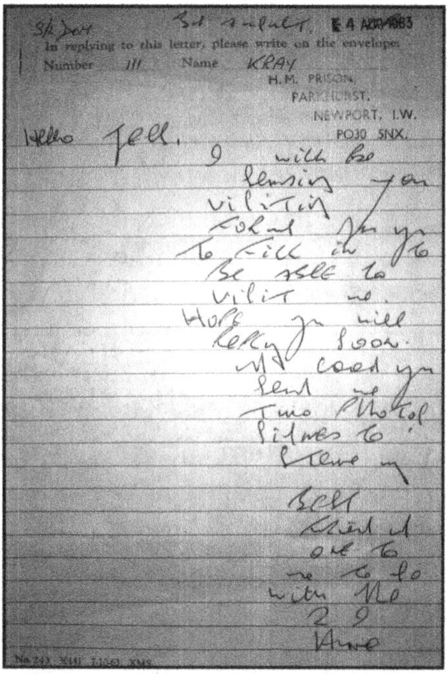

---

In replying to this letter, please write on the envelope
Number  111   Name   KRAY
H.M. PRISON,
PARKHURST,
NEWPORT, I.W.
PO30 5NX.

Hello Jell.

I will be sending you visiting order soon so you to fill in to be able to visit me. Hope you will reply soon. Will send you two photo of films to Clare my best kind love to me to to with the best love Ron

---

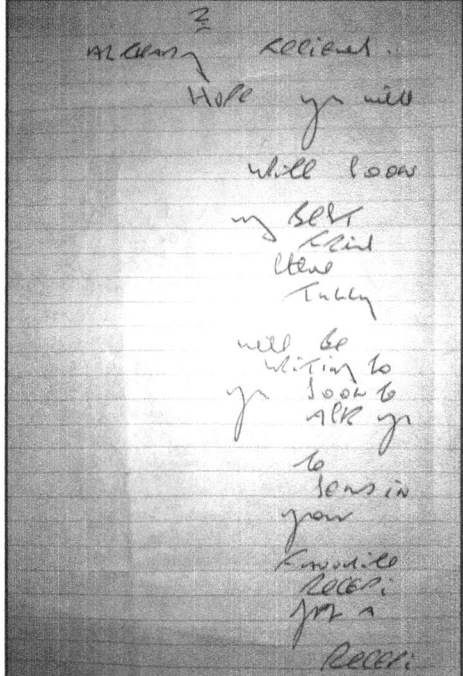

---

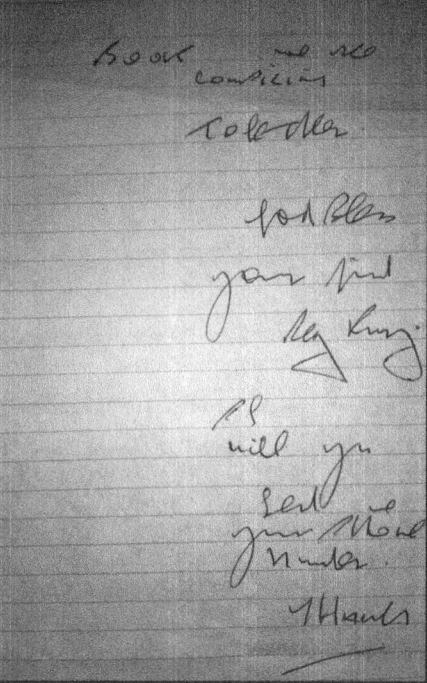

*Correspondence with Ronnie's brother, Reggie Kray*

There weren't CDs with backing tracks on so I had no choice but to take my band. When I told them that we were going to do a gig in Broadmoor they weren't too pleased. At the time they were paid £25 a week (which in today's money would be £175) and I told them they would get £25 for that one gig; they changed their minds immediately and said yes.

On the day of the concert, instead of dressing rooms we were offered two cells. I had the number 1 cell of course. There I was, in my tight-fitting catsuit, looking a million dollars in front of seventy-five inmates with broken noses and missing teeth, goodness knows what some of them had done or what they thought of seeing this. I did my opening number *Johnny B. Goode,* which usually ends with applause so loud that I have to do an encore. But at this performance, there was no reaction whatsoever. I stared out into the audience, with their cauliflower ears and broken noses, and there was stoney silence until Ron went, "Yeah!" and they all started clapping, and off we went for an hour or whatever with Ronnie starting off the applause at the end of every number. At the end of the show, Ronnie stood up and screamed for more and they all followed suit with a standing ovation.

Dors phoned and said your money's arrived. I got £5,000, which in those days was enough to not to work for the rest of the year, along with a thank you letter from Ronnie.

# 40: The 1980s & Are You Being Served?

In 1982, I played Robin Hood in *Babes in the Wood* in Swindon. Once again, I was back for the third time with Norman Vaughan who was starring as Merry Norman, *It Ain't Half Hot Mum's* Donald Hewlett, and Michael Knowles played the robbers. They loved me in Swindon and would often invite me back, and I didn't mind that as Dors was born there and she was always happy to come and see me, and with great panache sat in the box, and that always made the local press. Years later in 1991, I was honoured to be asked to return to Swindon to unveil a statue in honour of Diana Dors, along with her son Jason and Lord Puttnam.

After the success of me playing *Joseph,* on its second major tour – which happened to play the Gaiety Theatre, Ayr – they wanted me to be the first English star to play the lead in pantomime in Scotland. In 1983, I starred as Robin Hood in *Babes in the Wood.* The show was to co-star Lou Grant, who was a popular Scottish comic. I stayed at a luxurious hotel opposite the theatre with my family. The manager suggested we could stay free of

*As Robin Hood in* Babes in the Wood

charge on the understanding that I would perform cabaret for them on New Year's Eve. A good deal at the time as there were four of us on full-board. Pantomime is a big deal in Scotland and the runs are long. This show ran from 3rd December to 21st January, almost two months.

In 1983, I was asked to be a Special Guest Star in yet another iconic TV Series, *Are you Being Served?* I was to play the Head of the Sports Department, Mr Walpole. I was asked by the casting director whether I could play golf and of course I said yes. I am not sure where the role came from, as I was friendly with the creator & producer Jeremy Lloyd socially, and I also knew a fellow *Water Rat* Jimmy Perry, who was the writer. In any event, I was certainly well-cast.

The first day of rehearsal was all very friendly. John Inman was clearly thrilled that I was cast, as was Wendy Richard, although I could detect a possible half-smile from fellow pop star, Mike Berry. As always, Renée had packed my usual apple and sandwich for lunch, but as it was the first day of rehearsals and everyone was in good spirits, John and Wendy persuaded me to go for a drink with them, something they did every lunchtime. As I was first at the bar, a rarity, I found myself ordering drinks for everybody. I said to the barman, "I'll have half a lager and whatever Mr Inman and Miss Richard are having." He replied, "Miss Richard always has champagne." Not realising that it was a bottle not a glass that she had, I made sure the next day I went back to my usual routine of eating my pre-packed lunch and relaxing in the dressing room. Rehearsals went very well. Mollie Sugden was a joy to work with, as was fellow *Water Rat* Arthur English, whose Blue Plaque I recently unveiled at his house in Aldershot. I remember seeing Arthur English at the Brixton Empire back in the day, playing his famous cockney spiv with an outlandish large tie.

Once again, I made sure that my costume was up to my usual standard. To add to John Inman's comedy, in the scene where I wiggle my hips getting ready to demonstrate my golf swing, I made sure that my red golf trousers were tighter than tight. I went to wardrobe on the day of shooting where I was offered a choice of two golf gloves. Of course, I chose the more attractive one which was a white glove, as I knew it would be picked up better by the cameras. At the dress run, one of the chippies nonchalantly walking past us rehearsing, with a nail between his teeth, shouted over to the director, "I hope you realise your so-called golf pro has got his glove on the wrong hand!" It didn't even occur to me that this was the case, as I was more interested in the look, but if it hadn't been for that chippie, they would have shot the scene like that, and the show has been seen by millions of people and repeated for years ever since! Can you imagine the sacks full of mail that the BBC would have received!?

Working on *Are you Being Served?* was a great experience. John Inman and I had a tremendous amount of publicity, and he became a very close friend. We had so many happy times at his house in Little Venice and I was so sad when he died in 2007.

It's so great that the episodes are still being enjoyed today. I recently took part in a *Secrets and Scandals* documentary for Channel 5, on which I spoke about my memories as Mr. Walpole.

# 41: Dors Dies

By the time Dors had married Alan Lake, she had a child, Jason. Alan Lake didn't work much, owing to the fact he was an alcoholic. Lots of her loyal friends, including me, did wonder what on earth she was doing with him, because on many occasions when we went out to dinner together we would sit having a wonderful time chatting, having a bottle of wine, and he would be marching up and down the tables in a drunken stupor doing impressions of Adolf Hitler. Dors would say to me, "Look at him now, the silly bugger." Lake would threaten the waiters and management and act like a complete asshole. It was only because of Dors' fame that management would let him get away with it. It was a strange relationship to say the least. Dors saw him for who he was, but still stood by him to most of her friends' dismay.

I'd visited Dors at the BMI Princess Margaret Hospital in Windsor. A few days later Alan Lake phoned me up and told me Dors was dying. I got up there as fast as I could, and for some strange reason I had no trouble at all accessing her room, without being stopped by anybody or being asked anything. I remember going in and she was wearing a pink nightie, and she looked very beautiful. I got closer to her and realised that she'd gone. I thought about how cowardly it was of Alan Lake to just disappear and not to wait for me. He would later go on to shoot himself, so that when his son came home from school, he would find him.

I was closer to Dors than perhaps I'd been to any man. She really was something special. You talk about a moment in time, but it was one of the most tragic moments I've ever experienced. I finally got out of the hospital and there were, by that time, press outside. I had this feeling, just standing there, that it was the end of a chapter in my life that was important, but it was so sad and drastically showbiz.

It was such a big event in my life and other people's. The fact that this incredible icon, who was conflicting and complex but the most talented, perhaps underrated actress, yet liked to live her social life organising harmless silly pranks. She'd be in the kitchen, with a cup of tea going, and at times she'd remind me of my mum. She was also a mother-figure to Andrew Ray, and certainly Alan Lake. I suppose she did have that persona of being not only glamorous, but nurturing. You could say she was all things to all people. Yes, she was very promiscuous. Yes, she'd do anything for a laugh. Yes, she lived her own life, unapologetically. She acted exactly the way she wanted to act. She never ever changed the way she was to impress anybody. She was true to herself. What you saw is what you got. A glamorous person, full of fun. I never ever had a dull night out with her. Drama followed her. Laughter followed her. Tears followed her. It was a rollercoaster of life's ups and downs. Tremendous highs and tremendous lows. Even when she died, she looked beautiful in a pink negligee. She looked like the archetypal star. She looked peaceful. She looked glamorous. She looked like a star.

# 42: 1984 Panto

1984's panto saw me playing close to home. Not only is the Theatre Royal Windsor local, but it has the cache of being on a par with any theatre in the West End. Elizabeth & John Counsell were very famous for running the theatre for many years. *Cinderella* was to star Joe Brown as Buttons and Jess Conrad as Prince Charming. We had equal top billing and shared the number one dressing room happily together. Joe would later tell people that during the time we had spent sharing a dressing room in panto together, I never looked at him. Instead, I talked to him while looking at my own reflection in the mirror. He would go out for a walk between shows because I insisted on having my beauty sleep. I always took a sleeping bag with me and laid it out underneath the dressing room table. When I did my last panto, I sold the sleeping bag back on to raise money for charity.

The fairy godmother was Sheila Matthews. the Ugly Sisters were played by John Gower and Bryan Burdon, the son of the famous comic Albert Burdon who I worked with at The Grand Theatre Swansea. He was a fellow *Water Rat,* as was Joe Brown. It was a highly successful pantomime and I returned to the Theatre Royal Windsor for many more occasions, including panto and concert.

The rest of the 80s, it seemed that everybody wanted me to make guest appearances in their films without doing very much. In 1985 I guest starred in *Claudia*, which was produced by Michael Winner. In 1986, Julien Temple who, remembering me from *The Great Rock 'n' Roll Swindle*, once again gave me Guest Star billing in his latest film *Absolute Beginners*, where I remember newcomer Patsy Kensit took a shine to me.

# 43: The 1990s & the Punk and the Princess

In 1993, director Mike Sarne invited me to meet him in Soho as he had me in mind for the role of Rachel's father in a film he had written was going to direct, *The Punk and The Princess*. The film was based on a novel by Gideon Sams and was intended to be a modern-day *Romeo & Juliet* set in West London, involving a street punk who falls in love with a rich girl but their romance is frowned upon by their parents. A common plot in films.

Obviously, I knew Mike Sarne from his pop star days. In fact, when I was putting on a 60s show at the Theatre Royal Windsor for Bill Kenwright, Mike Sarne was one of the acts as he had found fame with the number 1 hit *Come Outside* with Wendy Richard. Mike had directed the likes of Mae West and Raquel Welch, and dated Brigitte Bardot, and I thought if he is good enough for them, he's good enough for me. How could I turn it down? I thought I could be missing something here. As it was a non-named cast, I thought that placing me as the father would probably be a good idea. Not only was I marquee value for the film, but I was obviously right for the part.

Mike never once used a studio, it was all filmed on location and my scenes were shot in a beautiful house with a huge inside pool, not far from where I live. So that was cushty cushty. The script was very good, and I had to do an American accent. On breaking the part down, I decided that it could have been played by Jack Nicholson. It had all his trademark characteristics. Apart from it being dramatic, I could see that there could be moments of comedy which I incorporated. Sometimes in films, more often than not, there's a character that is perhaps played by the girlfriend of the director or somebody concerned with the production. This must have been the case with the woman that played my wife, as she stuck out like a sore thumb. She was so bad, she made me look like Laurence Olivier! Although I never had a scene with the male lead Charlie Creed Miles, I was pleased to see that he became an actor of some note and although Mike Sarne may have made a mistake casting my wife, he certainly picked out a future star in him. Looking back at that film, I realise what a talented director he is. He has a great eye for detail.

Unfortunately, like most of Mike Sarne's films, *The Punk and The Princess* was regarded as an art house picture and therefore the film did not go into general release, although I'm told it has a cult following today, rather like another film I made, *Konga*!

In 1989, I once again guest starred, blink and you'll miss me, in a film starring Ray Winstone and Jamie Foreman directed by James Marcos called *Tank Malling*.

By now, I was employed in the movie industry based on my talent as opposed to me being the Golden Boy of the 1960s.

# 44: Sinderella

I was judging a talent competition in the 1970s sometime and one of the acts was a working comic called Jim Davidson, who I thought was the best comic of the evening, but the other two celebrity judges thought otherwise, and he didn't win. Being a great fan of the business, whenever I saw somebody that had the extra thing you need to become a star, I always took note of that person and would go backstage and tell them how good they were. I was so taken by Jim's performance, I felt that I had to go backstage and tell him. I knew that somebody in his position, which was a million miles down the ladder from where I was at the time, would appreciate the praise and

the fact that, in my opinion, he should have won the competition but didn't. I was, as usual, with two beautiful girls, wearing a fur coat which was then acceptable, but still outlandish. Very Liberace. Wearing a fur coat was OK if you could carry it off, and I could. But what impressed Jim Davidson more than the fur coat was the two beautiful models that were with me. I was right about Jim, and it wasn't long after that he hit the big time with own ITV series and specials, and Jim never forgot that compliment I gave him when he needed it most.

In 1985, hot on the heels of starring in *Joseph*, I got a call from the casting director Pat Hayley, who I knew very well as she was for many years Diana Dors' personal assistant. She was overjoyed to let me know that Jim Davidson wanted me to appear in his latest Thames Television special. Jim's idea was a sketch based around an all-star rock 'n' roll supergroup and he had enlisted the likes Hank Marvin, Rick Wakeman, Chas & Dave, Joe Brown, Roy Wood, and Francis Rossi. In the sketch, Jim introduces me as the "most fabulous singer he's ever seen in his life," and I come on, as a pastiche of a rock star, in a fur coat and sunglasses with a shiny silver suit and as I'm about to sing, my backing band consisting of the most famous musicians of the era all protest and walk off. The show was a great success, and Jim obviously saw something in me and enjoyed playing off my vanity. He continued to nurture this image of me in his future shows, including the pantomime *Cinderella* and many years later, *The Generation Game*.

Jim was looking for somebody to play Prince Charming, and in the end, he thought fuck it I'll get Prince Charming himself, me. Jim was the archetypal Buttons, and I was the archetypal Prince Charming, and he took *Cinderella* to the Alhambra in Bradford in 1989 and The Dominion in London's West End. When we were doing *Cinderella*, we'd always do a midnight matinee of what Jim would then call the blue version of the show which, oddly enough, was always packed with women in the audience. Jim later told me that he would go out front to watch my entrance flanked by pretty girls and as that worked, he realized the show would work, and that he had a hit on his hands. I could have told Jim it would have worked, as I'd been doing that type of entrance for years. What I didn't know at the time was that Jim was formulating in his head a bawdy version of *Cinderella*, *Sinderella* with an S for Sin, that he could tour in its own right; and that's what we did, playing places like the Shaftesbury and Cambridge Theatre.

Jim Davidson was always loyal to the people fortunate enough to be in his inner circle and used them again and again. One of his favourite Dames, who happened to be a very dear friend of mine, was Roger Kitter (codename The Doctor), who was a very fine stand-up comic and made an outrageous ugly sister. A lot of dialogue in *Sinderella* was made up of things like the slang for a man's manhood, The Corey, something that only the in-crowd in showbiz would be aware of. Wendell Corey, the Hollywood actor, was notorious for having the biggest manhood in the business. Legend had it that he could kneel down and knock a golf ball into the hole with it. Backstage, we had this enormous photograph of Wendell Corey that we paid homage to every night before the performance.

*Me, as Prince Charming*

Jim Davidson was codenamed The General by me, as he was very supportive of the army and still is to this day. We had so much fun on the show. Jim was very generous. There was a dressing room that was a bar, so that you could drink whatever you liked any time of the day you wished. If anything ever went wrong he would say in no uncertain terms that if it happened again, he would close the bar! In doing so, he kept a very tight ship.

Jim bought in the iconic Charlie Drake to play Baron Hardon. I was forewarned that Charlie Drake was very difficult, so much so that, at the time, he was virtually unemployable owing to his reputation, usually brought on by alcohol. But I've never known a comic idolize another comic as much as Jim Davidson idolized Charlie Drake. Jim gave Charlie carte blanche to do what he wanted, which I'm sure Jim knew all along would only ever enhance the comedy. When we started rehearsals, I ended up getting on wonderfully with Charlie Drake. We were both Cockneys, him being born in Camberwell and me in Brixton, and therefore Jim Davidson decided that I could be the one to make sure he'd get on stage every night for his first entrance. Jim arranged for a monitor to be installed in Charlie's dressing room so that he could see the show, which he did every night sipping his brandy, and it was my job to make sure that when he came out of his dressing room I would lead him to the stage for his cue. However, on one occasion, I got distracted by one of the chorus girls, and was deep in discussion as to whether we should go to *Stringfellows* for a drink that evening, and so I forgot to make sure Charlie got on stage. Consequently, he came out of his dressing room calling for the Primps, that's what he called me, and I was nowhere to be seen. On leaving his dressing room, and me not being visible, he turned left instead of right and found himself outside the stage door in the flower market. When I realized that I'd missed his cue, I went to check whether he'd made it to the stage, at which point Jim clocked me and made sounds like, "Where's the fuck's Charlie?!" Thankfully, by this time, the locals in the flower market had realized that Charlie needed pointing in the right direction and sent him back to the theatre.

Jim was ad-libbing for what must have seemed like a lifetime when eventually Charlie finally finishes up in the foyer of the theatre and chats up two of the usherettes, who realize he's in the wrong place and take him arm-in-arm down the aisle. Buttons, then seeing the Baron making his way towards the stage, goes into a wonderful comedy ad-lib that only Jim could have thought of on his feet. The audience were now in hysterics. The Baron finally makes it onto the stage, continues the scene, and makes his exit to the back of the stage where, instead of exiting, gets lost in the scenery and keeps reappearing while Jim is trying to continue with the show, which by that time has almost come to a standstill twice. Ad-libbing ensued once more, and the place erupted again. The interval finally arrived when, of course, I copped a bollocking from The General.

It was a tremendous opening night at The Cambridge, afterwards we all went to *Stringfellows*. Jim and I would often go there for steak in the evening after a show. The tour was a complete sell-out and broke all box office records. Not since *Hair* had the West End seen such a monumental success. Jim, never missing a trick, and being the great businessman that he is, made sure the show was a great success on video too, selling VHS copies in the foyer.

I kept in touch with Charlie Drake long after the show was finished, when he unfortunately ended up in Brinsworth House, the home for retired performers run by The Entertainment Artistes Benevolent Fund. Because of his lifetime of drinking and smoking, his deterioration was sadly quite rapid. By this time, the alcohol had taken hold and ruined his liver, and he was wired up, which was a very sad sight and made me very tearful. What made it worse was, he'd always try and tell me jokes and end up forgetting the tagline.

# 45: The Generation Game

By the mid-1990s, as I had such a close and successful professional relationship with Jim Davidson, it came as no surprise when he asked me to join him on his popular prime time Saturday Night show, *The Generation Game*.

At the time, *The Generation Game* was one of the most-watched Light Entertainment shows on TV. I had done three years with Jim in *Sinderella*, including two stints in the West End. We were almost known as a double-act. Jim thought it would be fun for me to be his sidekick. The idea was for me to play myself, Jess Conrad, who every week would try and get on the show and sing a song, with hilarious consequences. Jim would introduce me as Jess Conrad: the voice of Viagra, which became a catchphrase. I went on to use that intro wherever I appeared. On my entrance on *The Generation Game*, I would sing a couple of lines from a well-known song and then disaster would strike. One week, I came out and sang *My Way*. Before I could finish the line "and now the end is near", I would be blown up. Another week, I came out and sang *The Autumn Leaves,* only to have a gust of wind smash a window over my head while a leaf fluttered by. In the Christmas Special, I sang *I'm Dreaming of a White Christmas* in a long white fur coat, only to be covered up to my eyeballs in snow. The reason the character worked so well was that the audience knew that something dastardly would happen every week. They were one step ahead of the game.

Jim was completely hands-on. He cut things out that he thought weren't working, without consulting any other person. He directed things the way he wanted them to be. He thought he had a better grasp of comedy than the person giving him the note, which in fairness, he probably did. The reason he got the show in the first place was that they wanted to give the show a breath of fresh air.

I always enjoyed working with The General because no two days were the same. From laughter to drama, every day was different and you never knew what this brilliant showbiz brain was going to come up with next. Every day seemed to be a new adventure.

I had been on *Oh Boy*, *Wham!*, *Boys Meets Girls,* starring on Saturday Night TV prime time in the 1960s, and here I was thirty-five years later back on Saturday Night TV in the 1990s, performing to millions.

# 46: Telstar: The Story of Joe Meek

Joe Meek was the man that produced hit records in his bathroom. His biggest hit was *Telstar* by the Tornados which remained in the UK Singles Chart for twenty-five weeks and the U.S. Chart for sixteen. It was the first U.S. Number 1 by a British group. He was an incredible trailblazer. Nobody ever produced hit records in a home studio like he did in those days. So, he was a very unique record producer.

My best friend in the 60s was Michael Cox, who Joe had given a number one to with the record *Angela Jones*. So, I would often go up there with Mike because we always got a cup of tea, he was never on time for the appointment so we spent most of the day there just ligging about, as they say. The singer Heinz would sometimes appear from some mysterious place upstairs. Heinz was a one-hit wonder, with *Just like Eddie*. He was obviously Joe Meek's boyfriend, something that Heinz always denied, but I think in the end it turned him to drink to an extent where he was unbookable, and eventually drink killed him. I would always jokingly say to Joe that I would love to record with him and one day out of the blue he said he had a song for me. Heinz didn't like the idea of me coming into the stable. Great jealousy there, I mean I was a good-looking boy. One time, we were doing a show at the Walthamstow Empire and Heinz was on the bill. I was top of the bill and scored a run down on my first number, which meant all the fans got up from their seats and ran down to the front of the stage, which only happens if, as they say in the business, you tear them apart, which Heinz obviously hadn't. Afterwards, Heinz's roadie went to him and told him that I had stolen his act and I'd jumped on the amp. I now realized that Heinz never leaves a theatre sober, so he had plucked up some Dutch courage, barged into my dressing room unannounced, and accused me of stealing his act. I told him, "If it was going to nick someone's act, it wouldn't be yours, it would be Elvis's!" My pop star persona went out of the window and I got angry. I told him in no uncertain terms, "If you don't fuck off, you're going to get hurt." He didn't realise my background. I learned to look after myself at an early age and certainly knew how to fight dirty from my previous West End life. I knew he was going to get hurt if he didn't stop, but he didn't realise that and I grabbed him, pulled him towards me and nutted him, and then put him back against the wall, where he continued to rant and rave. So I thought, *fuck this, there's only one way to shut him up,* and so I bit his nose. I remember him squealing like a pig as he ran out of the room. I immediately had a mirror check and thought to myself, *perfect,* as I picked pieces of Heinz's nose out of my teeth.

Afterwards I wrote a letter to Joe saying I was sorry, and he wrote me a nice letter back to me and said more or less that he forgave me, and that boys will be boys. We then recorded *Hurt Me / It Can Happen to You* and he promised me that Sandie Shaw would duet with me. On the day of the recording, she didn't show up. So, Joe said, "Don't worry I'll do it for now," and went off. Halfway through the recording, he opened the studio door to give me a note and I saw he was wearing a woman's hat. A couple of years later, I was away filming and Joe was anxious to make another record with me. By the time the film was over, I received the news that he had tragically committed suicide.

Forty or so years later, the actor and filmmaker Nick Moran thought that Joe's life story would make a good film. So, in 2008, he happened to be at a theatrical lunch that I was attending. John Mills was there and stood up to address the room, after which I stood up and did something ad lib and tore the place apart. I topped John Mills and Nick Moran was in the room to see it. He was very anxious to get me to play the part of Larry Parnes in his new film, *Telstar: The Joe Meek Story and* spoke to casting director Kate Plantin about whether she could get Jess Conrad, and she did. I couldn't understand the reason why they wanted me to play Larry Parnes, as the only time I had met him was when he wanted to manage me. We'd met in the steak house in Leicester Square opposite the *Talk of the Town*, but I had turned him down because he had dandruff on his collar. The other thing I noticed was that he was a chain smoker, so much so that one of his fingers was so cigarette-stained it was brown.

Interestingly, playing Larry Parnes, it was the only time during the making of a film that I have been given real cigarettes by the prop man. Usually, even if I was playing gangster parts, they wouldn't allow me to smoke on screen.

The film told the story of Joe Meek's rise to fame and his struggles with debt, paranoia and depression which culminated in the killing of his landlady Violet Shenton and himself, on February 3rd 1967. When Telstar was made it turned my fight with Heinz into a comedy fight as I suppose, in reality, it was too shocking. Looking back, it was shocking. There is no question he had it coming to him, as I'd warned him until I was blue in the face, so he got what he deserved. Although obviously I would have preferred it not to have happened.

James Corden had one day on the film playing Clem Cattini, the drummer from The Tornados. James Corden had no idea how to play the drums, but at that time got the part as he was slightly rotund, like Clem Cattini.

Nigel Harman played me and was the type of actor that wanted to study the person he was playing, so he got in touch to ask if I would mind him coming to meet me. When he came through the door at my house, he looked so much like me, my wife Renée said uncharacteristically, "Are you sure your mother never met my husband?" One of the filming locations was the Richmond Theatre. I was put in the number 1 dressing room that I had often inhabited, being there with shows like *Godspell* in which I played Jesus, and Joseph in *Joseph and his Amazing Technicolor Dreamcoat*. It was an ideal location as I could commute from my home in Denham. Doing the concert scenes with *The Tornados* there was a nice location, and it brought back many happy memories of the time I spent there.

After we wrapped, the drinks party was at a bar on Great Marlborough Street, and I had gone outside for a cigarette just as the star of the film, Kevin Spacey, was on the way in. He crossed the road and walked towards me and cooed, "Hi Jess, I've heard all about you." Quick as a flash, I said to him, "You're not trying to pull me are you, Kevin?!" Not being used to being rejected, he changed his tack and asked me if I had a light, which I gave him, and he scarpered away, not in the direction of the party.

The film premiered at The Ritzy Cinema in Brixton, which was once known as the *Bug Hutch*, but was now the place to be seen in. I thought it was lovely, given my childhood spent there. Afterwards, some of the cast members including Nick Moran and Ralf Little had a nice meal in a restaurant that used to be the penny arcade when I was a kid.

# 47: The Last of the Summer Wine

Even the biggest stars in the business would welcome a guest appearance in an iconic show like *The Last of the Summer Wine*, and I am no different. My agent had secured Norman Wisdom for the part of Billy Ingleton, and in 2005 suggested me for a cameo, which director Alan J. W. Bell jumped at.

My closest friend at the time was Burt Kwouk, who was also in the series, and he was thrilled that I was going to take part. Burt lived on the Edgware Road and would get a coach from pretty much outside where he lived, right the way to Yorkshire where they filmed the series. Burt was known internationally for the *Pink Panther* Films, and I always wondered why such a big star would get on a coach, where he would inevitably be recognised, and travel all that way. He explained to me that it was ideal for him as it was an economical way to travel, and he also got to learn his script on the journey. I remember Diana Dors once telling me; never use public transport. When I asked why she said, "Do you think people would pay good money to see you in concert, if they saw you sitting on a bus!" It made perfect sense when she told me. Needless to say, I didn't take the National Express!

When Burt announced to his fellow cast members that his best mate, Jess Conrad, was going to be making a guest appearance, they seemed overjoyed, as they always did with any new member who would join their happy throng. I became part of a very important group of people who shared this honour.

I guest starred in the episode *Who's that Mouse in the Poetry Group?* where my scene was to involve a husband and wife hiking. When the director saw us together for the first time as a couple, he realised that although we were the same age and he'd cast us as man and wife, there was no way I could have played her husband. So, thinking of his feet, he immediately changed the roles to mother and son, which obviously didn't please the actress.

I became very friendly with Jean Fergusson, who I invited to many Heritage Foundation charity lunches, together with Juliette Kaplan. Brian Murphy has also been a dear friend over the years, along with my Variety Club Golfing partner, Russ Abbot.

# 48: Jess Receives an OBE

In 2011, I received the news that I was going to be gonged-up! I was to receive an OBE (Officer of the Order of the British Empire) for my charitable services over the years. Andrew Lloyd Webber was one of the first to call to congratulate me (I was his original *Joseph*), quickly followed by Bill Kenwright. To illustrate the variety of friends I have, the next call was from 1960s pop star Leapy Lee who had the number 1 hit *Little Arrows*.

The night before, my family were deliberating whether it would be The Queen or another member of the Royal Family from whom I would receive the OBE. The answer to that is, nobody knows until the ceremony.

On the big day, my dear friend John Griffin (founder of *Addison Lee*) arranged for me to have a limo take me to Buckingham Palace. I was delighted that I was in a position to be able to take with me my wife Renée and daughter Natalie, and her husband ex-Grenadier Guard Matt.

When my driver pulled up at Buckingham Palace, we were told in no uncertain terms that we couldn't go in the front gate. I said, "You don't realise who I am, I'm Jess Conrad and I've come for my OBE!" The guard said, "I don't care who you are, Sir, you can't come in this gate!" He then ushered me off to the other gate where we were stopped once again. I rolled down the window and said to the young-looking man, "My name's Jess Conrad and I'm here to receive my OBE," and he replied, "I know who *you* are, sir. When the Showbiz XI played the Metropolitan Police Football Team in Hampton Court, I saw my father put five past you. In you go..."

Every footman I passed on my way to the Ballroom, out of the corner of their mouths, said, "Alright Jess?" It was then it dawned on me that most of them played for the Royal Household XI and the Showbiz XI played them twice a year, once at Buckingham Palace and once at Windsor.

Before the ceremony, I was instructed on the Royal protocol. In other words, they speak to you, you don't speak to them, which is exactly what I didn't do of course! On the day of my OBE, Princess Anne was there to bestow this very special honour on me. She had a great sense of humour.

*My daughter Natalie lovingly looks on at Pops the Rocker, as she calls me, with his OBE*

She said, "I hope you're not disappointed I'm not the Queen." I said, "No, ma'am. As long as you're not disappointed I'm not George Clooney." Thank God she laughed, otherwise I'd be in The Tower of London!

Afterwards, I had arranged for us all to go to Mosimann's, one of the most prestigious private dining clubs in the world, for a celebratory dinner. The owner Anton Mosimann served us personally, which I must say made it a day I'll never forget.

I owe everything to my wonderful wife Renée who has taken a back seat, for all she's done to support me. I don't have an allotment and I don't go fishing. In fact, I don't have any hobbies. My entire life has been spent either working in showbiz or raising money for charity. I only have one regret. I just wish my mother was alive to see her Jessie Boy get the OBE. She would have been so proud.

# 49: Mob-Handed

In 1993, I met a double act called Ricky Diamond and Robert Hopkins when starring as the Sheriff of Nottingham in *Robin Hood* at The Millfield Theatre in Edmonton. The double act split up, and Ricky Diamond then changed his name to Liam Galvin and became a film director. Over the years, he stayed in touch and cast me in a kid's TV series called *Bodger & Badger* in which I guest starred as Mr Jelly. He also insisted that his wife Yvette Rowland co-starred in the series.

Then in 2016, Liam sent me a script for a gangster film he was making called *Mob Handed*, which centred around the story of a female journalist who joins a vigilante group after her daughter was murdered. Once again, his wife was cast, this time in the leading role of the vigilante journalist, which I was not aware of until the first day of filming. I was to play a judge who was a paedophile. It was as far removed as you could get from Joseph or Jesus, or any of the other leading roles I had played, and I agonised long

*Me at gunpoint*

*Me, playing the baddie for once*

and hard about playing such a controversial role. Then I thought, it is such a challenging part to play that it would be good for my fans to see me in a different type of role. The film was shot entirely on location and had an assorted cast of well-known actors. I must admit, Liam Galvin was a very fine film director, and I was very pleased with the way my performance turned out. Even I could not believe it was me. I had proved to myself that I could make an excellent baddie. The film ended up on DVD and streaming on Amazon, and was also recently seen on London Live. In 2023, Liam Galvin thought of me again to Guest Star in a film he was directing called *Somebody's Daughter*, the true story of author Zara H. Phillips's search for her biological father. I play the long-lost father. Having worked on the part, the author complimented me by saying her dad was just like that. The film is due to be released on Amazon and other streaming services.

# 50: Last Laugh in Vegas

I had become a pop star. I had become a matinee idol. I had become a musicals star. I had even been awarded the great honour of becoming King Rat of the Grand Order of Water Rats, whose past members have included Charlie Chaplin, Bob Hope, and Ken Dodd. I received my OBE from HRH Princess Anne, and now, in my eighties, I was about to become a reality TV star.

*Last Laugh in Vegas* came to me completely out of the blue, although I had always thought that I would have fitted nicely into *I'm a Celebrity Get Me Out of Here.* My dear friend, past King Rat, and one of the finest comedy acts, Roger De Courcey who by this time was also an agent, suggested me for a new reality show that would feature showbiz stars of the 1960s, 1970s and 1980s travelling to Las Vegas, to live together, explore the city and rehearse for a dream gig in one of the strip's most iconic theatres. I was then invited to have a meeting with the powers that be. I have always thought my persona is quite funny. It is so different from the real me that I was at loggerheads as to whether I should show producers the real me or my persona. I ended up showing them my showbiz persona, as I thought it would be amusing. I told them that I had never done a reality show before and it would be a first, and that I was very excited about the project. To my delight, I was thrilled to hear that they wanted me.

I was told my co-stars would include my dear friend Kenny Lynch, who I had met at the age of fifteen when we were both Teddy Boys in the West End. Anita Harris and I went right back to 1965 when we'd both been in the BBC play *Who is Mary Morison?,* a light entertainment fantasia on the life of Robbie Burns. I starred as Robbie Burns. The comic Mick Miller was an old friend of mine. When I was asked to organise an event called *Star Games* in Marbella, Mick Miller was one of the celebrities I asked to join me as I regarded him as one of the funniest acts I knew. He hated flying, but because we were good mates, he agreed to fly out. As he was so petrified on the plane, to give himself some Dutch courage; he got drunk, got alcohol poisoning then had to spend most of the week in hospital. By the time he came out, it was the day of the cabaret so he didn't get to play golf or enjoy any of Marbella. Bernie Clifton, who was famous for his ostrich, was somebody that I'd toured with for many years, he was in lots of the shows promoter Johnny Mans put together. I had the great pleasure of co-starring with Su Pollard in *Sweet Charity*, which toured England. I played the film star Vittorio Vidal and Su played Charity Hope, the role Shirley MacLaine made famous in the film. I'd known Bobby Crush, Britain's answer to Liberace, for years. We were close friends, although I always suspected he may have had a crush on me. The only stars I hadn't met were Cannon & Ball, who I'd always admired as a top-of-the-bill comedy act.

The first day of filming involved the cast all meeting each other at a venue in London to rehearse. The powers that be arranged that I would be the last one to walk through the door. They all treated me like I was top of the bill.

*Celebrating my* Last Laugh in Vegas *TV debut*

We were all then introduced to the Vegas show producer Frank Marino, who was the campiest thing we'd ever seen in our lives. When the cameras rolled, our first reaction was shock-horror at his over-the-top showbiz persona, complete with sparkly jacket, bouffant hair, and fully made-up. We were then told something had gone wrong with the camera, and that we would need to do our entrance again, and, of course, the second take showed our faces in a less startled manner. Marino was a Vegas producer type who would give us a hard time, but was really a very nice individual who just happened to be one of the biggest stars of the strip, which we weren't told at the time. The first thing Frank asked us to do, as he didn't know who any of us were, was to stand in a line in order of fame. Knowing I wasn't the most famous, I thought that it would suit my showbiz persona to say that I was. So, I stepped forward with my usual showbiz smile and aplomb to place myself at the head of the queue. I think from that moment, the TV producers realised that Jess Conrad wasn't going to go through the series unnoticed!

All nine stars were all reunited at London Heathrow Airport, full of high spirits. The contract stated that we would have first class flights to Vegas, luxury accommodation, and that all our meals would be supplied. We were therefore surprised to find that we flew economy and when we arrived we were housed in an imposing gated property some miles from the main Vegas strip. Having got up early and spent the whole day travelling, I was looking forward to going straight to bed and having a good night's sleep when we arrived, not realising that it was morning in Vegas and that we were expected to start filming immediately. We were all told to assemble in the entrance hall of the house, where I realised, for the first time, that the cameras were well and truly on us. This was reality TV.

Sleepy-eyed and slightly bewildered, we were then told in no uncertain terms that the rooms were upstairs and that we could now go and choose our own. So off we went. As I was the oldest, although probably the fittest, I was the first to get up the stairs. I got into the first room I could find, which was at the top of the stairs, and I checked and saw that there was a mirror and I said to myself, this will do me. So that was that. Bobby Crush was too slow to get up the stairs and found himself without a room, which I realised was all part of the plot, that somebody would be left without. The powers that be all knew that one person would be left out. They later found Bobby a room in the building adjacent to the main house but, having had time to think about it, he said in his interview on camera in front of millions watching at home, that I should have allowed the ladies to get their rooms first. When actually what the producers wanted was a mad rush and they knew somebody would be left out, and they knew that would make good television. In the end, Bobby got more airtime due to him unjustly complaining about it.

The next morning, I came down for breakfast wearing a dressing gown that I knew would look good on camera. As I arrived, I got a round of applause from the crew as if to say "here he is", it seemed I was the only one who made any effort at all which surprised me, after all we were making a TV series. Strangely enough, when I arrived there was a vacant seat at the head of the table where I sat down. They'd left the best seat for me. Although we were only wearing dressing gowns, most of which I would have thrown away years ago, it was obvious that I was the best dressed. I sat down and announced, to nobody in particular, "I usually have muesli for breakfast, but this morning I think I'll have a full English," and waited for whoever was serving breakfast to answer. Then somebody piped up, "There's no waitress service Jess, we have to do it ourselves!" To which I looked quite bewildered because I had never done it myself! My dear friend Su said, "Don't worry darling, I'll cook it for you," and dutifully served me a full English. She would also end up making my bed, as there was no person designated to do that despite the contract stating otherwise.

Then off we went to start our first day's rehearsal with Frank Marino. The musical director turned out to be a dear friend of mine, Andy Street, who I knew from my days on the musical *My Gentleman Pip*, the musical version of *Great Expectations* in which I played Pip. The musical premiered at The Royal Theatre Northampton in 1969, where Errol Flynn famously started his career in rep and is now rumoured to haunt. So, Andy being on show was a lovely surprise. We went to the rehearsal room where we were greeted by the dancers who were obviously all American. The rehearsals went as expected, which meant hard work for all, learning dance routines and going through our own spots with the MD.

We were informed one morning that there had been a terrible shooting at a music festival in Vegas where over sixty people had tragically lost their lives. The city had closed, as a mark of respect and the world was in mourning. It was decided that nobody in Vegas would work that day, but we had a dilemma on our hands. We were quite within our rights not to work, but, as we were on a tight schedule, if we took a day off, our show wouldn't open and everybody agreed with me that the show must go on. It was really chilling to look out of the window of the rehearsal room and see the hotel where the disaster occurred.

We finally arrived at the theatre where the show was going to take place that evening and I naturally shared a room with Kenny Lynch (codename

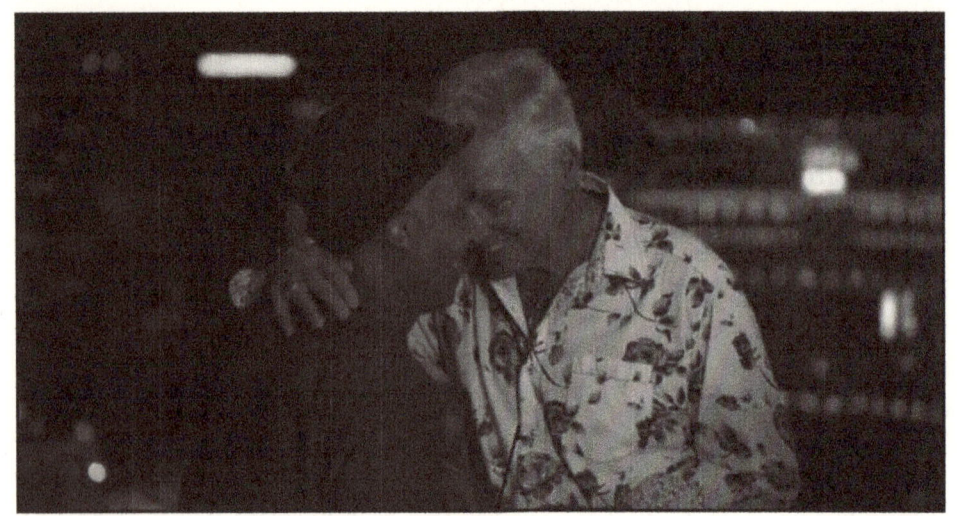

*With my dear friend Kenny Lynch*

Kipper). On one of the breaks, Kenny & I went out to the casino that was in the arcade just outside the theatre, and were over-awed by the scale of the gambling. We were happily putting our coins in a slot machine when a woman of a certain age came up to us and complained that we were using her lucky machine, as she'd been playing it for the last thirty years. I was disgruntled, but Kenny said, "Come on Jess let the lady have her machine," and we stepped away to let her back on it. It was as if nobody else was allowed to touch the machine other than her!

As usual, Kenny was so relaxed that even on the day of the show I literally had to wake him from a deep sleep to go on stage. The biggest shock of the show was the fact that we'd gone through all this palaver about working to an American audience, when in fact the auditorium was full of expats, who had come to cheer us on. The show went very well and I remember telling the audience, "I'm eighty-one and I've finally made Vegas!"

On our last night, some of the cast went to *The High Roller*, a big Ferris wheel with probably the best views of Vegas you can get. After a few drinks, Kenny & I started reminiscing about our friendship which had endured over fifty years. I leaned in to him and said, "If it all ends now, we've had a good time." Little did I know, this would be one of the last times we would be together. Within a short period of time, my dear friend would be gone and my heart would be broken.

# 51: Doctors

In 2022, I got a call out of the blue from my agent telling me that I had been offered a guest starring part in the popular BBC series *Doctors*. When I saw the character description, I realised the role was the complete opposite to me and I thought, my god this is going to be some acting job. It was obvious this wasn't going to be a walk in the park but I was surprised and delighted to be offered the role with no audition. In Episode 107 *A Safe Pair of Hands*, the description of Alan Yates in the breakdown was an anxious, shy character who has hidden behind his diagnosis of anxiety to retreat from society. Externally, he's trying to combat his cowardice by doing something brave. Internally, he's a victim who loves putting the world to rights, but only in his imagination. All of which was as far from Jess Conrad as you can imagine. The casting director showed so much faith in me that I'm still surprised that they did, but I now realise that they must have known that I could do the job.

I was taken up to Birmingham by my friend and manager Simon, as he was on his way to see his mother who lives nearby. We arrived at the hotel in Birmingham, the *Jury's Inn*, where I later found out that everybody in the cast stays, and when we got to my room I looked out of the window and said, "I don't like this room", to which Simon said, "What don't you like about it?" I replied, "I'm not happy with this view," to which he said, "This is Birmingham. What are you expecting, the French Riviera?!"

I was contracted onto the show for a week's work, but when I saw the schedule I noticed that all my scenes were crammed into two days. Day one were the interiors of what was to be my house, which incidentally was a real house. Then day two was all the exterior scenes shot outside in the street. I had eleven scenes in all, which was loads of dialogue. They worked at a pace that I'd never ever experienced in my showbiz life before, shooting everything with two cameras almost 'as live'. I realised then how much times have changed since I first started. Years ago this would have taken a week. Now, I was caught up in a whirlwind of dialogue, with no rehearsal, and all the director ever said to me was, "next scene, move." I did everything in one take unless there was a technical fault. Actress Sarah Moyle, who I played opposite, was very gracious towards me and put me at ease. After I'd finished, the producer came into my dressing room and thanked me, and insisted on me being chauffeur driven back home, as opposed to me going back on the train, which wasn't in my contract so she must have been delighted with my work.

I worked hard on the part but I had no idea until I saw the finished product just how I did. When I watched the episode air on 25th October 2022, I was really pleased with the way I had found a character and a voice that was not my own.

# 52: And Finally… Showbiz XI Football Team

I can't write a book a book about my life without an honourable mention of a very big part of my life, playing showbiz football.

When I was a kid during the war, there was no sport at school. You kicked a ball against a wall and that was the extent of it. In the late 1950s, I was in Legrain coffee bar, which had become a showbiz haunt, and Mike & Bernie Winters were talking about forming a Showbiz football team. Back then, they weren't as famous as they eventually went on to become, so they couldn't get a regular game in the Showbiz XI, and so they decided that they'd form their own celebrity football team. They would go on to call it the TV All-Stars.

In those days, there were three of four showbiz football teams the likes of The Entertainers Eleven, Showbiz XI, Top Ten Eleven etc. and we played for charity across the length and breadth of Great Britain to packed stadiums every Sunday. We would travel all over with fixtures in Scotland, The Isle of Wight, The Isle of Man, The Channel Islands and Jersey. More people came to see us than they did the actual football teams! Mike & Bernie were discussing what positions everybody would play and they got onto who was going to play in goal. At the time, there was a Russian goalkeeper called Lev Yashin who seemed to sweep through the air like Batman, dressed all in black, so I said, "I'll play in goal." Because I got to wear a different colour costume than anybody else, I thought, *that'll suit me*. When I got there that night, I said to mum, "Guess what mum. I'm playing in the showbiz football team. I need a pair of football boots." Now, I wouldn't know where to get a pair of football boots, but my mother knew all the tricks, and off she went to Woolworths and bought a pair for 2/6d. They were brown and had great big studs on the bottom. If you got kicked by the tip of the toe, you'd know all about it. Thus started my charity football career that lasted almost fifty years.

I started with the TV All-Stars and then new celebs came along like Rod Stewart, Ray & Dave Davis of the *Kinks*, Dave Dee of *Dave Dee, Dozy,*

*The team's star keeper*

*Beaky, Mick & Tich*, and Junior Campbell of *Marmalade* fame. By the late 1970s, Mike & Bernie had split up, so I was asked to take over running the Showbiz XI football team, which I was thrilled to do. I've always been good at organizing, so it came naturally to me. When I was a Teddy Boy, I had my own group called *The Black Hand Gang* and mothers would come to my mother and ask if their sons could be a part of my gang. They'd say, "My son's a bit of a wimp, can he come and play with your boy?" So I was always a leader-type. I was sponsored by Ford, who gave me a car so long as they could have 'The Showbiz XI sponsored by Ford' emblazoned on the side. On the plus side, I didn't have to buy a car for fifteen years! So obviously we would play the Ford factory team. We'd also play Metropolitan Police twice a year at Hampton Court, and the Royal Household at Hyde Park and Windsor. We had lots of regular games like that, where we'd play the same team once or twice a year.

One time, I was booked by Jimmy Savile to take the Showbiz XI team up to Leeds. I'd met him once before, well before he found fame, when he booked me for a personal appearance up north at the Mecca Locarno Ballroom in Leeds. I went up by train and was met at the platform by Jimmy – all gangstered-up, flanked by two minders... quite a sight! By this time, Jimmy was a part of the showbiz scene; everyone knew him. He wasn't a West End boy like me, he was very rooted in Yorkshire. He was talkative, loud and would always be the main attraction – you'd never see him without his cigar. After the Showbiz XI match, he invited me back to his, where we had tea. When he was showing me around, he took me into what turned out to be a bedroom and proudly opened the wardrobe. He said, "These are all my mother's dresses. Aren't they lovely?" Slightly bemused, I nodded and politely agreed saying, "Well, yes they are". He then asked, "Would you like to try one of the dresses on?" I replied with an instant, "Fuck off!" as I thought he was having me on... but the fact that he thought I'd put one on shocked me. I didn't think any more about it at the time – I dismissed it as some kind of gay thing. It was only later that I realised just how strange what he was asking me to do actually was; Norman Bates in Psycho comes to mind! He was a real oddball – though I must admit I could never have predicted the many horrors that would later come to light.

Lady Sheila Butlin, widow of Sir Billy Butlin, founder of *Butlin's Holiday Camps,* would book us every year and arrange a private plane and first-class gourmet dinner for the team. We even went as far as Majorca, which I loved so much, Renée & I spent a lot of time there. All the Spanish games were organized by my good friend, 1960s pop star Leapy Lee, who by then was

*With Ronnie Corbett, Larry Taylor, Tommy Steele, Alfie Bass,*
*Pete Murray, Mike & Bernie Winters… and more!*

living there. We would always have great names kicking off the match for us, the likes of Barbara Windsor, Shirley Anne Field, Faith Brown, Glenn Ford, who is the nation's number one Norman Wisdom impersonator, and Chris Greener, who was the tallest man in England at one time. When we went to Majorca on a private jet, which only sat a dozen or so people, Chris Greener would have to be pulled by his arms into the plane and lay down in the aisle during the flight! When Chris Greener kicked off for us, ten minutes into the game, Ronnie Corbett, the smallest member of the team, would be sent off by the referee. We always did it as a recurring gag. The ref would gesture "You're off," pointing at Ronnie, and Ronnie would have a mock argument about the decision, at which point Chris Greener at 7ft 6¼ would appear, towering over the ref and dwarfing Ronnie, gesturing by wagging his finger that if the ref didn't let him stay, he'd have to deal with him! A bit of showbiz schtick!

The Showbiz XI football team was comprised of the likes of Tommy Steele, Anthony Newley, Alfie Bass, Bernie Bresslaw, Pete Murray, Harry Fowler, Kenny Lynch and myself. All big names in the day except for a then unknown Sean Connery, who was a chorus boy in *South Pacific*, and hadn't yet had his big break. Over the years names like Rod Stewart, Roy Castle, Freddie Starr, Dennis Waterman, Ray Winstone, Robbie Williams, Phil Daniels, David Hamilton, Jimmy Tarbuck, Stan Boardman, Lonnie Donegan, Malcolm Roberts (Hit Record – *Love Is All*), and Des O'Connor would join the team. The team started training in Hyde Park, but before long, as most of the boys at the time were Arsenal fans (Mike & Bernie Winters and Pete Murray), we were invited to train at Arsenal in Highbury. It was common practice that lots of famous retired footballers loved to play for the Showbiz XI, as football is a part of showbusiness. Bobby Moore was a regular player, as were George Armstrong, Ron Atkinson, Dave Beasant, Martin Chilvers, Dave Bassett, Billy Wright, Vinnie Jones, and Paul Gascoigne. There were no egos in the changing room. We were dedicated, taking risks and making sacrifices that today's stars wouldn't dream of.

I earned quite a reputation as a shot-stopper, bravely diving in and risking my heavily insured teeth at the same time. As part of my role as organizer and manager, I would design the logos, source the sponsors, negotiate with the FA, and arrange packing the laundry and travel. When I was making movies like *Aliki* in Greece, *Hell is Empty* in Czechoslovakia, and *The Golden Head* in Budapest it was written into my contract that, every Saturday, wherever I was, I would be flown back to London Airport to play. I also kept a record of every match and every score because, apart from a bit of rehearsal schtick, it was proper competitive football. We were deadly serious when it came to the result. At the beginning, we didn't know which way to go so we thought we'd give the public what they wanted and do a bit of comedy football with buckets of water over the head and silly hats. But it really didn't work. What we soon realized was, what they wanted was a good game of football played by their favourite celebrities. They turned up in their thousands. In May 1957, singer Alma Cogan kicked off a Showbiz XI game at West Ham in front of 23,000 people, but crowds often reached over 30,000. We always drew more than the local team.

Every week we'd play for different charities, from the Aberfan disaster to the Bradford Fire, Hillsborough to Dunblane, local hospices and special schools, Save The Valley, the Wishing Well Appeal, community centres etc. I kept a list of charities, and the money we raised over the years was hundreds of thousands of pounds. My tireless devotion to charity, until a rotated cuff forced me to quit playing in The Showbiz XI in the 1990s, ultimately earned me my OBE (Officer of the British Empire) in 2013. Not bad for a cockney kid from Brixton.

# 53: Charity Golf

The whole concept of celebrity golf started with the Rat Pack. So now, you can't be a celebrity and not play golf. Charity Golf is a bit like football. Everybody did it, so I realised I had to do it; and, of course, I looked good in the gear. I was well-sponsored. All the leading sports brands wanted to dress me. So, although I may not have been the best golfer, à la Jimmy Tarbuck, I was always the best dressed and obviously the best looking.

I mean, a lot of people say golf is a very expensive sport. Not for me. I've never paid for a round of golf in my life! I wouldn't even know what a round of golf costs, but every time I picked up a golf club, I was raising thousands of pounds for charity.

Over the years, I played every major golf course in Great Britain, from Gleneagles to Wentworth. The first time I played Wentworth, I stayed over and they gave me the suite which overlooked the first tee. I woke up in the morning and looked out of the window, and it dawned on me that I was a number 1 celebrity in the best suite in Wentworth overlooking the first tee, and that's how it went on.

For a lot of the people who play golf, it's a feather in their cap if they play for a well-known charity with a well-known celebrity. The teams would comprise a celebrity with three ordinaries (non-celebrities) and there would be twelve teams or so in a game. Members of the public pay big money to play charity golf with celebrities. Whilst raising money for worthwhile charities, they're getting to spend the day with a well-known celebrity. So, it's important to be good company, which I've always been. They love the bunny. What's normal to me in my life, is exciting for them to hear about. As I love talking about myself and my famous friends – male and female – they love hearing my stories. A day's charity golf would include breakfast, a round of golf followed by drinks reception, dinner, and cabaret performed by whichever star was headlining that day. I've played with big American stars like Telly Savalas, Howard Keel, and Bob Hope as well as British favourites Michael Parkinson, Ronnie Corbett, Russ Abbot, and Sean Connery.

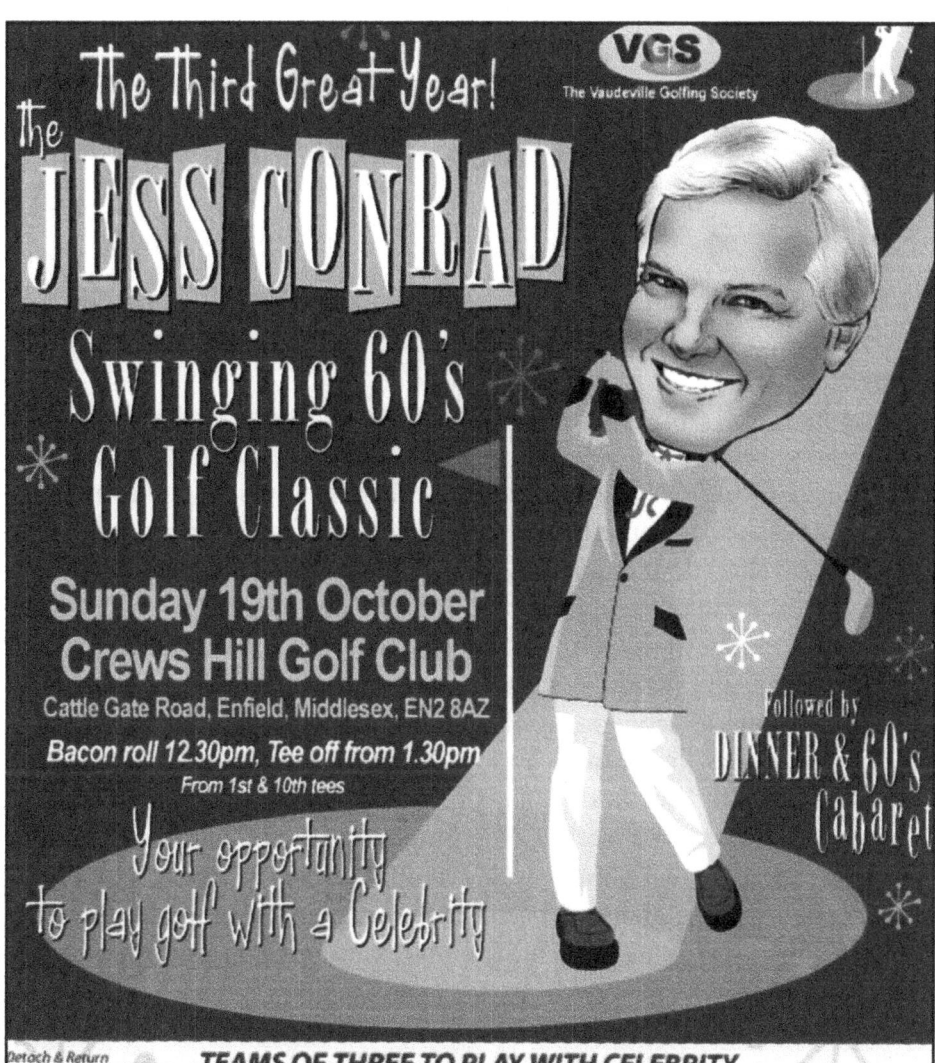

The Third Great Year!

**VGS**
The Vaudeville Golfing Society

# the JESS CONRAD

## Swinging 60's Golf Classic

**Sunday 19th October**
**Crews Hill Golf Club**
Cattle Gate Road, Enfield, Middlesex, EN2 8AZ

Bacon roll 12.30pm, Tee off from 1.30pm
*From 1st & 10th tees*

*Your opportunity to play golf with a Celebrity*

*Followed by* DINNER & 60's Cabaret

---

*Detach & Return*

**TEAMS OF THREE TO PLAY WITH CELEBRITY**
*Your Celebrity to be drawn from the hat on the day*
**Team of Three £225 or £75 per Player** (to make up a team)
*4 Ball Stableford, Full Handicap, Best Team Score*

Player's Name ............................................ Handicap ............

Player's Name ............................................ Handicap ............

Player's Name ............................................ Handicap ............

*Please enclose a cheque made out to VGS £ ............ in payment for ............ Players*

# 54: Grand Order of Water Rats

My father was a mason and I followed in his footsteps, being given the freedom of the city of London. I can walk my sheep over London Bridge whenever I wish!

Then in 1986, I was made a Water Rat, which was a great honour. The tradition is pure showbiz. Lots of people want to be Water Rats but they don't always make the grade. You have to be a really good person, and somebody that can bring the coins into the Water Rats coffers where we raise money for the under-privileged. The Grand Order of Water Rats has been going since 1889, when the music hall circuit was in full flow. It exists as a wonderful Fraternity and Charitable Organisation, providing support for nationally recognised charities, whilst embracing the benevolence of their members, families, and our showbusiness colleagues. We hold meetings at the Water Rats pub on Grays Inn Road, Kings Cross. Over the years, Past King Rats have included Will Hay, Bud Flanagan, Tommy Trinder, Frankie Vaughan, Danny La Rue, Bernie Bresslaw, Roy Hudd, and perhaps most famously, Bob Hope. In 2013, that honour was bestowed on me.

I was made King Rat at a star-studded ball at the famous Lakeside Club in Essex, guests including Roy Hudd, Tom O'Connor, Ron Atkinson, Bobby Davro, Steve McFadden, and Margaret Whittaker OBE, founder of *Slimming World*. I asked Lesley Joseph, who was one of my disciples in *Joseph*, to accompany me at the top table. However, due to work commitments, she wasn't able to attend. So, her friend Maureen Lipman DBE took her place. Before which, they must have had a conversation about what I was like. Lesley Joseph must have been far off the mark because I got the impression Maureen Lipman thought she was on a date. But of course, she wasn't. Then she went home early. But it was nice of her to come.

*OK! Magazine* covered the event and in the video, hosted by Lizzie Cundy, Dame Barbara Windsor says of me, "I've known him forever, ever, ever, ever. And I remember the first time we got close was at Diana Dors' funeral. We were both invited onto breakfast television. Because he was

very, very friendly with Di Dors," to which Lizzie says, "He's very popular with all the ladies," and Barbara replies, "Oh I know but look at him. He was and still is the most handsome guy ever." In fact, after Dors died Barbara Windsor became my closest female friend. Although Barbara Windsor always thought I was in bed with Dors all the time and I think she was a bit worried I didn't make a move on her. But over time we became great friends, inseparable, like Dors. I was always at *Tramp* with her and had some great times there.

# 55: Celebrity Friends – Cliff Richard

I first met Cliff when he was cast in his very first film *Serious Charge* in 1959, and we became very good friends then which has lasted up until the very present day. This would be my last appearance as a film extra. I became a student of the Actors Workshop, went into rep and became an actor and, by chance, a popstar myself with some success.

We were part of a gang of Teddy Boys. He played the part of Curly, for no apparent reason, and always jokingly complained that he had to be there an hour before the rest of us to have his hair permed.

Around that time, we were pictured at the birthplace of rock 'n' roll, the *Two I's Coffee Bar* on Old Compton Street in Soho.

We met at numerous celebrity functions over the years, including a particularly interesting occasion when Cliff was sporting a beard, owing to his role at the time as Heathcliff in *Wuthering Heights*.

Another time, I was invited to go to Elstree Studios to celebrate Cliff's *Summer Holiday* films.

I was asked to participate in *An Audience with Cliff Richard* for ITV where I asked him, "As one heartthrob to another, how do you keep your youthful good looks?" which put a smile on Cliff's face and caused great laughter, and got me a round of applause from the audience. Then I pointed at my chin and I said, "A lot of people think this is my dimple, it's actually my belly button! I've had everything pulled up."

*Cliff and me at his Variety Club 60 Years in Showbiz bash*

Most recently, I was invited to be with Cliff by The Variety Club of Great Britain to celebrate his 60th Anniversary in Showbiz at the Marriott Grosvenor Square on 11th July 2019.

Cliff always invited me to his shows, but unfortunately I was either on tour with Jesus in *Godspell* or *Joseph and the Amazing Technicolour Dreamcoat*. But my wife always went with my two daughters, Natalie & Sasha.

# 56: Celebrity Friends – Freddie Starr

I was on tour with *Joseph* and Bill Kenwright had put Belfast up on the board as our next tour date. At the time, it was considered a dangerous place to go, there was a doorman on every door, not many shows ended up there. But, of course, our show went everywhere. We were told in no uncertain terms, "Don't ever discuss religion."

I went home every weekend on the first flight on a Sunday morning, on what I used to call the flying sausage. I would get standby tickets. But one time, just before I was about to get on the plane from England to Belfast, a bunch of children arrived and the powers that be let them go on first. So, there was no seat left for me. So, I had to get the next plane which meant I would miss the opening by fifteen minutes. I wrongly or rightly phoned Bill Kenwright and explained to him what had happened, so he could hold the curtain, only for him to reply, "You must be fucking mad," [to chance not buying a ticket]. But there always seemed to be plenty of tickets if you went standby, and the difference in price was worth taking the risk. When I got to Belfast, the taxi driver explained that he was going to take me down The Fall's Road, a road nobody went down. It was considered dangerous, but it was the quickest way to get from the airport to the theatre. Every second counted. Thankfully, the taxi driver had the nous to pick up my *Joseph* costume from the stage door, so I changed in the cab. I went straight on stage, with no makeup, which was a first for me. Then, every time I came off stage, I applied more makeup. So, by the end of the show I ended up with a completely different face to how I started it. The audience must have thought, every entrance I made, the character was getting younger!

I was in my hotel room in Belfast one morning, having a mirror check, and I saw Freddie Starr's face in the mirror behind me! I obviously thought I was seeing things. How did he get into my room? Freddie was a dear friend who I'd known for years, but seeing him looking at me through a mirror in Belfast was a shock to say the least. Shocking people was a part of his character, as anybody who knew him well could testify. It turned out that

he was appearing next to the theatre down the road, and not doing very good business, whereas *Joseph* was a sell-out. He wanted to see the show, but there were no seats. But because he was a friend, and Freddie Starr, I asked the management if it would be possible to allow him to stand backstage and view it from the wings; and because I was top of the bill in a hit show, whatever I wanted they would do.

That night, halfway through the show there's a scene where Joseph is in a loin cloth in chains in prison and mimes climbing up an imaginary wall singing *Close Every Door to Me*, and I always received a standing ovation at the end. On this particular night, at the end of the song, instead of receiving my usual round of applause, I received a very different reaction. Kind of a mixture of laughter and applause. Realising that something was amiss, I looked to my left to see Freddie Starr bollock naked wearing only shorts with swastikas on! I looked at him in shock horror and he said to me, stuttering in his inimitable style, "I've come to h—h—help you". When the commotion finally subsided, Freddie departed stage left telling the audience, "My name's Freddie Starr, appearing next door, seats at all prices."

# 57: Celebrity Friends – Norman Wisdom

Every now and then you get what they call special action, which means you have a few lines and do something that could be given to a qualified actor. If you suit the part, you can do it as a film extra and get a special action fee. I did that in a film called *Follow a Star* in 1959 in which I played a Teddy Boy who heckled Norman Wisdom on stage at The Metropolitan Theatre on the Edgware Road. That's where we first met. The second time I met him, the situation changed. I was then a name, and was sharing top billing with him in a touring show. By this time, Norman wasn't always coherent. More often than not, I would go into his dressing room to say hello and he would be surrounded by fan club members, led by the president, whichever country they were from. They would sit there looking at Norman looking as if he was god-like, looking in amazement at the great man. One day, I went in there to see him and he was alone. I told him, "You've made lots of famous movies, haven't you? And you've starred with lots of famous actresses haven't you"

"Oh yes," he agreed. Then, almost out of nowhere, he exclaimed loudly, "I sucked Joan Crawford's cunt, you know!" I immediately stood to attention and saluted him and said, "Well done, sir!" On reflection, I thought to myself it must have been a true story, as if it wasn't, he'd named somebody more attractive like Marilyn Monroe!

Towards the end of Norman's long and illustrious life, he was looked after at Brinsworth House, the residential and nursing retirement home for theatre and entertainment professionals. One day, Norman wandered off and found himself at the local petrol station, which was opposite a shopping centre. Upon being recognised by one elderly lady, Norman as per usual went straight into his act, attracting a sea of onlookers which were building every second. Before long, the petrol forecourt was packed with elderly ladies carrying their shopping and being entertained by Norman Wisdom. The man running the petrol station, having no idea who Norman Wisdom was, realised that he was of a certain age and probably from Brinsworth. He phoned Brinsworth to say that there was a person from the home who stopped him from selling his petrol. After a few minutes, somebody from the home came over and took Norman's arm, only for him to reply, "Don't take me off, I'm doing well!"

# 58: Celebrity Friends – Tom Jones

At my dear friend Kenny Lynch's funeral, which attracted so many showbiz personalities like Michael Parkinson, Jasper Carrot, Harry Redknapp, and Tarby who was the master of ceremonies, Tom Jones arrived and we embraced saying how nice it was to see each other. After the funeral, at the reception, I reminded Tom that when we first met in the 1960s, he'd had his first hit record and we were coming out of Club dell'Aretusa on the Kings Road. I was carrying him out of the club with Leapy Lee, who at the time had a hit record called *Little Arrows,* and I said to Tom, "Now that you have a number 1 hit record, you've got to smarten yourself up. The first thing you've got to do is get some new daisies[3] and get your bugle done." Later on, he pulled me aside and said, "That wasn't the only time we met Jess. Don't you remember you took me home from a Dors party in your red Jaguar? I was so impressed, I went out & bought one the next day!" I thought to myself, either he has a photographic memory or I'm somebody who you never forget!

---

3. Daisy Roots = Boots

# 59: Celebrity Friends – Lionel Blair

When I first met Lionel and his sister Joyce, I was at the height of my popularity. Around that time, NME had dubbed me Britain's Most Popular Singer over Cliff Richard and Adam Faith. So, I was riding high. I had been booked for the lead role in Play of the Week, *Someone who Cares*, alongside Vivienne Martin & Beryl Reid. Incidentally, that was where I first met Anita Harris, who has been a very close friend ever since. Lionel Blair and his sister Joyce featured in one of the dance routines in the play.

In the early 1970s, Joyce and I toured in a play called *Romance* alongside Bill Simpson, star of *Dr. Finlay's Casebook*. I'd pick Joyce up at Watford Gap, where she would leave her car for a week, and we'd drive up north in my car. Joyce would be there waiting for me in the car park, made up looking the full Marilyn Monroe. The play later went into the West End at the Duke of York Theatre on Shaftesbury Avenue. Joyce and I struck up a close friendship, mainly because she wanted a close friendship. She fussed over me and mothered me and made sure I was happy. After rehearsals, we'd go and see Lionel. She'd take every opportunity for the three of us to get together. She'd parade me in front of him, as if I was a trophy, knowing it would antagonise him. Over the years it would seem as though Lionel and his sister Joyce were always jockeying over which of them had the closest friendship with me. It almost seemed to be a competition.

When we first met, I was very famous and Lionel was starting out. He got famous by Mike & Bernie Winters taking the piss out of him on their many appearances on Sunday Night at The London Palladium, like Jim Davidson did with me on the *Generation Game* and in *Sinderella*. Lionel eventually became a persona in his own right and he used me in all his shows. I guested on *Give Us a Clue* and he directed me very well in panto. Lionel wasn't a famous stage director. So, when I was told he was going to direct *Goldilocks and the Three Bears* at The Wimbledon Theatre in 1974, a panto never done before or since, I was interested to see how well he would do. I played a character called Hank the Yank and got Special Guest Star

billing. I had an entrance where I walked through the door onto the stage and went into some sort of dialogue. We rehearsed it, and it seemed to me to be a very throwaway entrance and I was worried about whether I would get a round of applause. In pantomime terms the star should always get a round of applause on their entrance, but it has to be well-staged. I said to Lionel, "It's an unknown pantomime and I'm playing a character that nobody has ever seen before. I'm a bit worried about this." At the dress rehearsal, which a select few were invited to watch, I came on and, as I thought, there was no reaction. So, I said to Lionel. "See, there you are. This is the first time I've ever been in panto and not got a round of applause on my entrance." So he said, "Don't worry darling, I'll fix it," and he immediately arranged for one of the chorus girls to pre-empt my entrance by bursting onto the stage exclaiming, "It's Hank the Yank, he's on his way!" It was as if she was introducing Elvis! So, I swept on to the stage and got an enormous round of applause, and that was all through Lionel's ability to understand all the elements of stagecraft.

Lionel and I were friends for well over sixty years. He always approached me in company and greeted me like we had a very special relationship, which we did have. Whenever we were company, he always seemed to over-do it, by putting on a showbiz display. Whereas, if he came into a room and it was just the two of us, he wasn't anywhere near as animated.

I don't know anybody in showbusiness that didn't know that Lionel was bisexual. I remember once being at a showbiz charity lunch and Lionel's wife got onto the subject of us actor-types, saying how we were all that way inclined. I said, "Now, hold on just a minute. I'm not!" To which she replied, "Lionel told me you *all* are!"

# 60: Diamond Wedding Anniversary

People ask me, "When are you going to retire?" and I say, "You don't retire in showbusiness, the phone stops ringing." Well, in my case, the phone is still ringing. In February, I enjoyed a sell-out gig at The Phoenix Arts Club in London, hosted by Misty Moon Events, where I talked through my career accompanied by film clips. Some of my showbiz friends Su Pollard, Vicki Michelle, and Patti Boulaye were amongst the stars there that night to show their support.

I've also guest starred in *Somebody's Daughter,* directed by Liam Galvin, and the American movie *Mantopus!* directed by Joshua Kennedy. *Mantopus!* revolves around an insane movie director who, in his quest to create the most realistic monster movie ever made, hires a half-man half-octopus to star in his production. Chaos inevitably ensues. The film is a throwback to the horror films of producer Herman Cohen. I was cast in a cameo as the newsreel announcer and given the same character name from *Konga*, Bob Kenton. The film will be available on Blu-ray and Amazon Prime.

Then, in August, Renée & I celebrated our 60th Anniversary in our new house in the garden of England, Kent. Over one hundred guests, all showbusiness personalities, attended our garden party overlooking our beautiful lake. The koi carp were a talking point. I'm told they're worth £1000 each! All said and done, not bad for a South London boy.

So ends the incredible life and times of Jess Conrad; popstar, 60s Icon, and all round show-off. All my life, I have only ever read showbiz autobiographies. Gee, I hope you have enjoyed reading mine.

*My manager Simon interviews me at the sell-out Misty Moon event*

*My daughters Natalie and Sasha at our 52nd wedding anniversary garden party*

# Jess Conrad Discography

## SINGLES

| | | | |
|---|---|---|---|
| 1960 | Cherry Pie | Decca | F11236 |
| 1960 | There's Gonna Be A Day | Decca | F11236 |
| 1961 | Out Of Luck | Decca | F11259 |
| 1961 | Unless You Mean It | Decca | F11259 |
| 1961 | Mystery Girl | Decca | F11315 |
| 1961 | The Big White House | Decca | F11315 |
| 1961 | This Pullover | Decca | F11348 |
| 1961 | Why Am I Living | Decca | F11348 |
| 1961 | I See You | Decca | F11375 |
| 1961 | Oh You Beautiful Doll | Decca | F11375 |
| 1961 | Every Breath I Take | Decca | F11394 |
| 1961 | Walk Away | Decca | F11394 |
| 1961 | Hey Little Girl | Decca | F11412 |
| 1961 | Twist My Wrist | Decca | F11412 |
| 1962 | Pretty Jenny | Decca | F11511 |
| 1962 | You Can Do It If You Try | Decca | F11511 |
| 1963 | It's About Time | Decca | F11620 |
| 1963 | As You Like It | Decca | F11620 |
| 1962 | Swimming In Tears | (Unreleased) | |
| 1962 | Didn't Want You Too | (Unreleased) | |
| 1962 | You Can Kiss Me If You Like | (Unreleased) | |
| 1963 | Take Your Time | Columbia | DB4969 |
| 1963 | I Know You | Columbia | DB4969 |
| 1964 | Pussycat | Columbia | DB7223 |
| 1964 | Tempted | Columbia | DB7223 |
| 1965 | Things I'd Like To Say | Columbia | DB7561 |
| 1965 | Don't Turn 'Round | Columbia | DB7561 |
| 1965 | Hurt Me | Pye | 7N15849 |
| 1965 | It Can Happen To You | Pye | 7N15849 |
| 1966 | A Little Bit Of Loveliness | Pye | PY133 |
| 1966 | Tin Pan Alley Rag | Pye | PY133 |

## SINGLES (cont.)

| 1969 | The Other Side Of Life | President | PT269 |
|------|------------------------|-----------|-------|
| 1969 | See The Tinker Ride | President | PT269 |
| 1969 | A Conspiracy of Cards | (Unreleased) | |
| 1970 | Crystal Ball Dream | President | PT292 |
| 1970 | Pussycat (Different song to DB7223) | President | PT292 |
| 1971 | Here She Comes Again | President | PT357 |
| 1971 | My Idea | President | PT357 |
| 1971 | Don't Lock Me Up | (Unreleased) | |
| 1974 | These Are Not My People | Antic | K11508 |
| 2016 | Seven Nights to Rock | (Unreleased) | |

## ALBUM TRACKS

| 1961 | That's My Weakness Now | Decca | LK4390 |
|------|------------------------|-------|--------|
| 1961 | You Too | Decca | LK4390 |
| 1961 | Rag Doll | Decca | LK4390 |
| 1961 | (I Wanna) Love My Life Away | Decca | LK4390 |
| 1961 | Little Ship | Decca | LK4390 |
| 1961 | An Angel Cries | Decca | LK4390 |
| 1961 | Just The Two Of Us | Decca | DFE6666 |
| 1961 | Maybe You'll Be There | Decca | DFE6667 |
| 1961 | It Tears Me To Pieces | Decca | DFE6702 |
| 1963 | It's About Time (Alt. Version) | Decca | DFE8524 |
| 1963 | I Don't Care What People Say | Decca | DFE8524 |
| 1963 | One Of These Days | Decca | DFE8524 |
| 1963 | Down Home Tonight | Decca | DFE8524 |
| 1976 | Be Bop A Lula | SRT | CUS046 |
| 1976 | First Thing Monday Morning | SRT | CUS046 |
| 1976 | Without A Worry In The World | SRT | CUS046 |
| 1976 | Dizzy Miss Lizzie | SRT | CUS046 |
| 1976 | Give Me A Star | SRT | CUS046 |
| 1977 | Save It For A Rainy Day | EMI | EMI2682 |
| 1977 | Lock Up Your Daughters | EMI | EMI2682 |
| 1977 | Hey Little Girl (Alt. Version) | EMI | EMI2682 |
| 1988 | Johnny B. Goode/Carol/Little Queenie | HAPPY FACE | LPMM1037 |

# About the Co-Author, Simon Withington

Back in 1999, I was twenty-five year old television researcher working on a now long-forgotten show for LWT called *40 Years of Freddie Starr*, which saw Britain's wildest and best-loved comedian celebrating forty madcap years of showbiz in a pacey, prime-time hour of music and comedy.

The producer of the show, Paul Lewis, wanted to capture some of Freddie's closest showbiz pals hurling insults at him to play into the programme. He envisaged a friend who he'd wronged saying things about what a devious rascal he was, thus getting their own back on him on his special night. So, I was hastily dispatched with a DV camera, then new technology – much like a camcorder but broadcast quality – and I single-handedly filmed the likes of Faith Brown (who famously had 'maggots' thrown at her by Freddie, much to her horror, at his *Audience With* a few years earlier), Vince Hill (famous for his *Edelweiss* hit and somebody who had plenty to say about Freddie), and the actor and singer Jess Conrad.

When I arrived at Jess's house in Denham, the man himself was there waiting for me. I must have been late (a terrible trait of mine that continues to this day) after filming Vince Hill up the road in Shiplake, Oxfordshire. As Jess stood there, all 6ft 1 of him, at the entrance to his house, Bambi Lodge to greet me, his lower half was covered by a stable-style door. But his top half – the important bit – was resplendently kitted out, casual yet the height of showbiz glamour, in cowboy tie with pearly white teeth and his trademark smile. He was camera-ready. Well, let's face it, when is he not?

I filmed Jess in his lovely garden and when we finished, Jess bid me farewell insisting that I must film his Showbiz XI football team sometime. I had no idea what the Showbiz XI football team was (anyone who knows me knows that sport is my least favourite topic) and I must admit, I knew even less about Jess Conrad. Remember, this was long before the age of the internet.

That evening, I called my mother and excitedly told her about all my adventures with famous people that day. When I mentioned Jess, as he'd made quite the impression on me – he has this effect on a lot of people, I now know – my mother explained that although she was a Rolling Stones girl she, of course, remembered Jess from back in the day.

Fast forward a couple of weeks and I found myself at a big glitzy party at The London Studios for the then Controller of Entertainment Nigel Lythgoe's fiftieth. Along with all the LWT Entertainment staff, the showbiz soiree was a veritable who's who of on-screen talent, with the likes of Cilla Black and Shirley Bassey putting on the glam to celebrate the much-loved Nigel's landmark birthday. I was in the little boy's room when I heard a voice say, "So when are you going to make that documentary on my showbiz football team?!" It was Jess, who I later learned was a dear friend of Nigel's (Nigel had directed him in *Babes in the Wood* Panto). Struggling to think in the heat of the moment as to why I hadn't followed up Jess's previous invitation, I hastily promised I'd be in touch.

Now, I am blessed in being a good all-rounder; I film, I edit, I produce, I direct. I don't quite write the theme tune, but if push came to shove, I could! After I cut a sizzle tape for Nigel in the then disused Studio 10 Edit Suite, which I happened to have the entry code for having worked there a few years earlier at Granada Talk TV, Nigel insisted I should be hired on some of LWT's most popular and exciting shows. My career trajectory was on the up. So, when Jess and I started filming our *Day in the Life of Jess Conrad* documentary, it took about five years to finish it! I fit filming in between jobs and after hours. Bit by bit, we shot scenes of Jess talking about his long and illustrious career and personal life, we filmed at a concert, at his panto at the Millfield Theatre, at a Showbiz XI football match playing in goal (as he "liked to wear a different colour outfit to everyone else"), raising money for charity playing golf, and revisiting his old stomping ground in Brixton ("dressed very ordinary so I don't stand out"). We also secured contributions from some of his lifelong pals including Tom O'Connor, David Hamilton, Shirley Anne Field and Norman Wisdom. His wife Renée also described seeing him across a crowded room and thinking *that's the man I'm going to marry*. All gold. The documentary was sold at Jess's concerts and later on Amazon.

Over time, our friendship blossomed. Jess gave me the codename (all his best friends have a codename) 'Smiley Boy' on account of my positive outlook. I attended the Conrads' thirtieth Wedding Anniversary, which was held at Sir John Mills' house in Denham with a stellar cast of guests including Juliet Mills & Maxwell Caulfield, Robert Powell, and Anita Harris. At that event, I presented Jess with a VHS cassette tape of his 1967 movie

*Hell Is Empty* which I'd lovingly tracked down with some clever detective work. I've since gone on to find most of Jess's 'lost' films including *Aliki My Love*, shot on the island of Ios, after I organised a meeting with Finos Films at their offices in Athens during a trip to Greece. Together we've enjoyed Heritage Foundation lunches (at one Christopher Biggins asked, "Where's Renée?" to which Jess replied, "I've got Simon." For years, Jess insisted that Biggins was probably jealous and hence not talking to him anymore!), trips to the theatre, and I've latterly become Jess's manager, securing him movie gigs and dealing with the everyday running of his social media, which includes a Twitter and Instagram account.

During lockdown we started penning Jess's memoirs. Socially distancing, we'd sit at either end of Jess's log cabin in his Denham garden (which I call "the hut", much to Jess's amusement) and we'd diligently go through Jess's career step by step, with me acting as chief secretary and fact-checker. We found several dusty manuscripts penned as pitches to publishers back in the day, which helped as an aide-mémoire. The trail of people who had tried to tell Jess's story at one point or another in Jess's career, lay by the wayside. I found the whole experience truly bonding. I'm happy to say I now know exactly who Jess Conrad OBE is; his contribution to pop culture, the constant reinventing of his career (from pop star to movie star, to television star, to theatre star, to reality star, to icon!) and I have a renewed respect for his success which spans eight decades and counting. During an airing of *Last Laugh in Vegas* at his daughter Natalie's house, I recall exclaiming to Jess, "You were on prime time TV in the 50s and you're still on prime time TV in the 2010s!" He's been there and done it all and he's still here. To me, Jess is a true star of the golden age of showbusiness. But more than that, he's my closest friend and somebody who I care deeply about. Now, there may be another book about a showbiz icon who always wanted a son, and a fatherless boy who dreamed of working in TV. But, that's for another time…

Simon Withington
January 2024